# Your Million Dollar Network

*How To Start And Build
Your Million Dollar Network*

**by July Ono**

On The Beach Education® Corporation
Delta, BC, Canada

Library and Archives Canada Cataloguing in Publication

Ono, July, 1962-
Your million dollar network : how to start and build your
million dollar network / by July Ono.

ISBN 978-0-9811127-0-1

1. Business networks. 2. Business communication. 3. Success
in business. I. Title.

HD69.S8O56 2008        650.1'3        C2008-906255-8

Illustrations: Kristell Clair, KickStart Communications Inc.
Editing & Layout: Cathrine Levan, KickStart Communications Inc.

Printed and Bound in Canada
First printing: January 2009

10  9  8  7  6  5  4  3  2  1

## Praises For Your Million Dollar Network

"As a result of networking and building relationships the right way, my net worth has increased by more than 200%."
- Irene Dong

"If I had known just how rewarding it is to produce a regular newsletter, I would have made it the backbone of my marketing plan when I first started my healing practice."
- Alice Brock

"My newsletter has been absolutely crucial from a real estate business perspective but also great from a social perspective as well."
- Eric Choi

"This newsletter stuff really worked and was so effective that by the end of June I was invited to be a part of a Joint Venture team."
- Hilke Krug

"Social currency in networking is not in how many people you know, but how strong your relationships are."
- Alice Zhou

"I find having a newsletter a very efficient and quite personal way to stay in touch with people."
- Paula Marinescu

"I feel that over the past months my readers have been walking side by side with me on my journey in real estate investing."
- Christian Gaulin

# Acknowledgments

This book is dedicated to Steve Cain, the love of my life and an ever present support. It's his persistence and insistence that helped me start my newsletter. His unwavering belief in serving others by giving value and staying connected, is far more valuable than any business plan or corporate agenda, as the true path for making millions in whatever you do. He taught me that in everything we do, it's all about relationships.

And I must thank my mother, Sumiko Urata, for being the social butterfly that she is. She served as an excellent role model for this budding networker. I witnessed her unswerving dedication to helping others in her community and forging bonds of friendship that last to this day.

And I would like to express my heartfelt appreciation to all my students, who provided valuable feedback in helping me to refine the essential components. I learned as much in the teaching as in the doing.

# Foreword

The best publicity often happens in the most unexpected places. Guerrilla publicity is about promoting yourself and your message, and this book describes how to do just that. People do business with people who have taken the time to get to know them, understand their needs and provide what they need even before they think they need it. It's about building relationships from your heart and soul.

Relationships are your most valuable asset. It's great to network, but then what? You need a system to capitalize on your networking efforts in order to be able to monetize them. July has bridged the how-to gap. She walks you step-by-step through the process of creating an effective continuity program.

Relationships are built on trust and *Your Million Dollar Network* shows you how to build trust, and your business, more effectively.

- Jill Lublin

International speaker, master strategist, radio and tv host, best selling author of *Guerrilla Publicity, Networking Magic (Adams Media)* and her latest book, *Get Noticed Get Referrals (McGraw-Hill)*
www.jilllublin.com

# Table of Contents

Foreword .................................... 5

Introduction ............................. 9

## Section One

Build Yourself A Continuity Program .......... 15
What Is A Continuity Program? ............... 15
Getting To First Base ......................... 21
Making It To Second Base ..................... 22
Getting To Third Base ......................... 25
Hitting A Home Run ........................... 26
Checking Your Response Ratio ................ 27

## Section Two

Building Relationships ....................... 33
Why Do I Need To Build Relationships? .... 36
The Value Of Cultivating Your Network .... 38
3 Degrees of Separation ..................... 41
Set A Goal .................................... 45

## Section Three

Do I Really Need A Newsletter? ............... 49
Expanding Your Comfort Zone ................ 52
Networking With A Purpose ................... 60
The Purpose Of The Page ..................... 63
The Power Of The Page ....................... 68
What Is Stopping You? ........................ 70

## Section Four

How Do I Get Started? ........................ 77
The First Step ................................ 78
What Do I Call My Newsletter? ............... 86
How Many Pages Do I Have To Write? ...... 86
How Do I Section My Newsletter? ............ 89

# Table Of Contents (continued)

## Section Five

| | |
|---|---|
| Putting It Together | 95 |
| Your Tools | 96 |
| Keep Your File Small | 98 |
| Formatting Your Newsletter | 100 |
| What Do I Write About In My Newsletter? | 103 |
| The 3-30-300 Formula | 105 |
| Make It Interesting—Use VAK Words | 109 |
| How To Deal With Writer's Block | 119 |
| Too Much To Say? | 120 |
| Wait Before You Click Send | 124 |

## Section Six

| | |
|---|---|
| The Launch | 131 |
| Organization Is Key | 132 |
| Psychology | 138 |
| What Happens Now? | 143 |

## Section Seven

| | |
|---|---|
| What's Next? | 147 |
| Your Marketing Program | 148 |
| The Energy Cycle | 150 |
| Corporate Identity For Larger Databases | 160 |
| Branding Your Business | 160 |
| Getting Noticed | 162 |
| Taking It From Here | 163 |

## Appendix

| | |
|---|---|
| Recommended Reading | 168 |
| Testimonials & Newsletter Samples | 170 |
| About The Author | 192 |

# Introduction

"If you're going to meet people anyway, you might as well get rich doing it . . . and the sooner you start, the better."

- July Ono

This book could be worth millions of dollars to you because it was designed to help you raise millions of dollars. I wrote it to show how you can build and monetize a network of 200 people to over 2,000 within two years. I developed the plan and did just that.

Quite often people ask me, "July, where do you find partners? Where do you find money?" As soon as they ask that, I wonder if they have a continuity program.

So I ask, "How do you follow-up with the people that you meet?" Well, they don't. They usually make a phone call here and there, or "Let's do lunch," and then they lose touch.

When people approach me for help with growing their investment business, the first thing I do is help them set up a system to stay in continuous contact with the people they meet. Most people don't have a continuity program, and that is why they have no money. People only give money to people they trust. And when the amount they are asking for is in the hundreds of thousands of dollars, you have to have a lot of trust and rapport built up for them to give you that kind of money. Money is

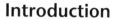
People only give money to people they trust.

emotional. It shouldn't be—but it is. As a result, you have to work against years of programming for someone to part with their hard earned money because their emotions are attached to the whole concept of money. After all, it's not just money, it's about trust.

Leveraging relationships is the key to acquiring real capital.

What you might not understand is that the size of your network is in direct proportion to your net worth. When I knew 20 people my net worth was negative 40,000 dollars. After I started building my network up, suddenly my net worth started increasing as well. How is that possible? Well, think of it like this, the more I surrounded myself with like-minded people, the more I started thinking like them and vibrating at their level. It's like a tuning fork that resonates at a certain pitch—you start to draw other people to you, in essence becoming a people and money magnet. *Your Million Dollar Network* is about how you can start to become a money magnet. Instead of chasing after money, wouldn't it be a lot nicer to have money chasing after you?

When it took all of 45 minutes to raise one million dollars for a real estate deal, it became very apparent that leveraging relationships is the key to acquiring real capital.

Building your network is easy, once you know how to do it.

In the beginning it is always tough, because you are just starting to build your network. People ask, "Who are you? Are you a real estate investor now?" How do you convince people that you are serious about this? This is one of the reasons why I developed the concept of the newsletter. It became too labor intensive to write individual letters and send cards each month to keep in contact with everyone. The cards didn't have enough meat and the letters took too long to write out. With a newsletter, right from the get-go we can share what's happening in our lives, keep potential investors in the loop, inspire people to take action, and provide the most important thing of all—value, value, value.

Right away I discovered that people crave story over facts. A good story is the binding agent that draws in the reader. Facts are boring, sterile things that really don't reveal a person's character or motivation. Isn't this a lot of what you see at networking events? A whole bunch of people going around spouting off facts about their business. Where's the connection in that? And in this life it's all about connecting. The cliche "It's not what you know but who you know," is a fact. Nepotism rules!

The reason is simply because friends and family are more familiar than strangers. Remember that most people fear the unknown. There is

> People crave a good story over facts. Tell your own story.

no point of reference, and it takes a lot of effort to discover if someone is who and what they say they are. A referral from someone you trust and respect has greater credibility and accessibility. Connected people have preferred status. So stop being a stranger. When you find someone you connect with say, "Here's a copy of my latest newsletter for your reading pleasure . . . and by the way, welcome to the family."

When we were first starting out we knew that there had to be an easy way to keep up with people every month. There is, and it's so simple and powerful that I can't believe that everyone isn't doing it. Maybe you are not computer literate enough to start, maybe you are scared that people will think that you are not smart enough or have interesting enough stories to tell. None of that matters. I am here to tell you that building a million dollar network is easy, once you know how to do it. And once you start you will wonder why you never started this sooner. It's all about managing and following up with the people you meet. The fortune is in the follow-up . . . and the follow-up . . . and the follow-up.

# Section One

## Your Continuity Program

# Section One

## Build Yourself A Continuity Program

As I said earlier, your net worth is in direct proportion to your network. Networking is a vital component of your business and marketing strategy. It supplies new connections to your business with people who, at some point, may be willing to invest in you, and with you. Building that foundation of trust requires maintaining regular contact with them. If you don't have a continuity program and are networking regularly, you are literally throwing money away.

If you don't have a continuity program why even bother taking someone's business card at networking events? Results only come from following up and having a continuity program. If you fail to plan, you plan to fail. If you fail to follow-up, you plan to fail. Every successful entrepreneur, business owner, and salesperson knows the value in following up. It is the defining difference between failure and success.

## What Is A Continuity Program?

A continuity program is designed to keep you in regular contact with the people you meet and know. This is your million dollar database whether you realize it or not. Establishing your continuity program is a critical business building and social building skill, not just for today, but for

*Following up is important. People need to feel they can trust you before they do business with you. So, Follow-up!*

tomorrow. As I mentioned previously, it's not "what" you know per se, that's important, but "who" you know, and who they know. The people who they know, that also know you, are even more important.

A continuity program helps you to build:

- Trust
- Credibility
- Consistency
- Reliability
- Dependability
- Professionalism

It's amazing how very few people follow-up. Having a continuity program puts you a step ahead of the average networker. It sets you up for success like no other single marketing strategy can.

Your continuity program is designed to cultivate quality relationships. It's not a quick-fix to get business, it is a long term commitment. The goal is to give more value to your subscribers by sharing your values, your expertise and unique experiences. It's about you, and it's also about giving value to others to help improve their lives. If you do it right, you endear people to you. And be careful, because if you do it wrong, your reputation will suffer. I have learned the best ways to do it, through trial and error, and will show you what to do and how to do it, so that you have the best possible chance for success.

> A continuity program is not a quick-fix to get business.

To help you get a better understanding of what I am talking about, I like to use a baseball diamond analogy to draw a clear, mental picture of the process.

Most people run around collecting cards from everyone they meet at networking events. I call this Home Base because this is where most business cards end up: at home in a shoebox. So let's start there, and move through all the bases:

**Home Base:** Networking—you meet people, screen them, establish a rapport and start collecting cards

**First Base:** Suspect—you follow-up to see if they are interested

**Second Base:** Prospect—they express interest but no sale

**Third Base:** Client—you make the sale

**Home Run:** Evangelist—they bring you more sales because they believe in you and want you to succeed.

## Running The Bases

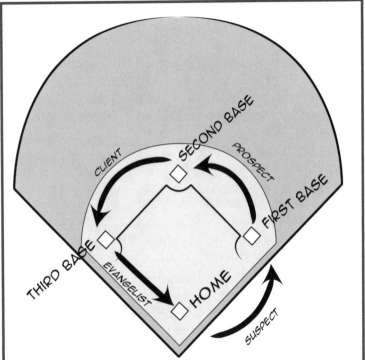

*Your goal is to move clients from suspect (first base), past prospect (second base), and buying customer (third base), to evangelist (a home run). At that point your network will start growing your business for you.*

On a baseball diamond, you start at home base. Most people go to a networking event and pretty much just stand around, so they are standing at home base with their bat, ready to swing. And the ball (a prospect), comes by and they don't even swing. What is that about? Why would you even go to a networking event and not network? So the thing is, at least get to first base. Get out there and hit the ball or at least swing at it when the ball (a prospect), comes towards you. Opportunity is all around you. It's coming at you all the time. What are you going to do about it? The ball is coming. Take a swing at it. Yes, you will miss some of the time. Babe Ruth struck out way more often than he made home runs (1,330 strike outs to 714 home runs). The thing is, eventually you will hit. You might get a base run or maybe even a home run.

So what do you do now that you have taken a swing and have ended up with a business card and potential lead? When you manage to get a few leads, take the time to add them to your database and follow-up. You will then spend a lot of time and effort following up these leads. At first, these people are suspects. They suspect your motives. They suspect your product or service. They suspect your reputation because they don't know you. If you manage to get past first base, these leads become prospects, if and when they express interest in your product or service. This is the lookey-loo phase. It will take more work and coaxing on your part to get them interested in parting with their money.

> Collecting business cards is like hitting a good pitch in baseball. Once you have a hit, you have to run to make it to first base.

If you manage to get past second base, they become clients. Hooray! You've made a sale. This is where most people stop and then start the process all over again. But wait a minute. You're not on the score board yet. Getting to third base is great, it's taken a lot of effort to get here, but what you really want is the home run.

You may wonder how it seems possible that some people are able to create effortless marketing, advertising and promotion with almost no budget. This is because they have turned their prospects into evangelists. I call it "hitting a home run." It's what you have been waiting for. When your clients have an awesome relationship with you, they preach the good news about you, your product or service to everyone they know and they do it all for free because they love you. Evangelists are worth more than gold. Third-party (evangelist) marketing is a very powerful tool because word-of-mouth is still the most potent form of advertising. Start looking at how you can turn your clients into evangelists. This process begins by collecting business cards.

In order to get a home run, you have to turn your client into an evangelist.

When you get home from an event, make sure you follow-up immediately. If that is not possible, then do it, within 24 hours. It can be as simple as, "Great meeting you, here is my newsletter as promised, and let's stay in touch."

Establishing rapport is about building trust with people through regular communication, on a consistent basis. If you are not consistent in your communication with potential clients, it will take you a very long time to build trust with them and even longer before you become successful. The secret to every business success is follow-up. So if you want your business to succeed, make sure you do your follow-up.

I like to stay connected to everyone I meet. I pre-qualify them when I shake their hand. If the rapport is there, I ask if they would like a copy of my newsletter. It is essential that you always ask permission to send it. Your newsletter must be permission based. Never spam people. Spamming people is the quickest way to ruin a good reputation. We always think less of someone who spams. Even if your intention is to inform, only do that *with permission.* And don't try to sell anything in your newsletter. In all sincerity, your intent must be all about, "How can I help you?"

The rules of the ball game are simple. To be a World Series Champion, you need a winning strategy vs an ineffective strategy. Watch the pros—successful people, model them and you will get similar results. If you want to win, model a winner. So let's walk the bases as we learn the tools that will get us into the World Series of building your million dollar network.

## Getting To First Base

When you first meet someone and start up a conversation, things will always pop up. Write them down on the back of their card. Pay attention and make notes. People like to be heard. It shows you care. I usually take preemptive action and say something like, "I hope you don't mind my taking notes. It works better than my short term memory." I jot down a little blurb about our meeting with a few tidbits from our conversation thrown in to keep it fresh in my mind. Listening is a lost art. This is your edge, so make sure to take notes.

The first e-mail you send to them always takes the longest because you are formulating your response and reviewing your conversation. It can take 10 to 20 minutes, or longer, just for a single e-mail. Don't worry, this is normal. And you know what? It's worth it if that one person says, "Wow this is amazing—she actually cared about what I said and gave me a suggestion for something of value. I want to see what else she is about." Value, value, value. Keep putting it out and they will keep opening your newsletter.

There are people who have been in my database for four years, and although I may not directly remember who they are, they continue to receive value from reading my newsletter every month. I help them by providing advice and guidance, or if they need a certain resource I might point them in the right direction. My goal is to become a trusted "go to" person. This is part of what keeps them in relationship with me. Ask yourself what you can offer your database.

<table>
<tr><td>Card Front</td><td>Card Back<br>*likes skiing*<br>*has a dog named Sammy*<br>*looking for investments*</td></tr>
</table>

*Write key information on the back of the business card to help you remember important details when you go to follow-up.*

## Follow-up

Always follow the 24 hour rule or the 48 hour rule. Follow-up with new contacts within 24–48 hours of meeting them. Become a fanatic about this. I mean it! This is a non-negotiable rule. The chances of you following up after 48 hours are almost nil, so don't put it off by saying you'll do it the next day, or in a couple of days. Do it now. Interest cools, and if you wait until the next week, you will be more distant in their mind. Then you have to start building rapport all over again. It's just not worth it to wait.

Okay, so let's say you make it to first base with your contact—the prospect stage. You have established rapport, interest, you have exchanged e-mails and that is about it. This is when they start to express an interest in your service, in your product, in you as a person—but there is still no sale. How can you get them to second base?

## Making It To Second Base

As a general rule of thumb, around 5% of the people in your database are ready to buy now, 90% are not ready or are waiting, and 5% will never buy. Knowing this, you have

*Are they ready to buy now?*

to understand that your network needs to be cultivated.

When your suspect turns into a prospect, they are not quite ready to do business with you. They may still have some resistance to jumping right in to work with you. You will probably have to do some more trust building before they are ready to engage. This is a very important stage because it sets the foundation for the future. During this time, your job is to work subtly on two types of strategies: the Convincer Strategy and the Motivation Strategy.

The Convincer Strategy is to simply repeat the same message over and over until the person is convinced through repetition. Television commercials are quite effective at this but aren't very affordable.

Some people are one application convincers. They see something they want, they hear about it or have a strong gut feeling and they buy right then and there. I would categorize these types of people as impulsive or compulsive buyers. Then there are the multiple application convincers. They need to hear the message 3 times, 5 times or 30 times before they will buy. By the way, the majority of people don't know they have a convincer strategy. We all have it, and we react without even being aware that we are acting it out.

We all have a Convincer Strategy, and react to it without being aware of it.

I was introduced to Scott by someone in my network, when I had asked them for help finding the best database management software. I followed up with Scott by e-mail and we corresponded. We even chatted on the phone once. That was about it. In the meantime, he subscribed to my newsletter and received it every month. One day Scott showed up at one of my seminars. I recognized his name because I have a talent for remembering names and e-mail addresses. He became a client that night and I looked up his contact information. Sure enough, we had spoken 3 years and 36 newsletters ago. His personal Convincer Strategy took 36 repetitions before he acted. He was now ready for a change in his life and I was in the forefront of his memory banks. I was a familiar face to him, with regards to real estate investing, so he thought to himself, "Why look anywhere else?" My newsletter did the work for me, and moved him from a prospect to a client. It's so simple, and the results are simply amazing.

> His personal Convincer Strategy took 36 times before he acted.

The second strategy is the Motivation Strategy. There are two types of motivation Strategy: Towards and Away. Think of it as the carrot and the stick. Some people are attracted by the carrot (the reward) and some people are attracted by avoiding the stick (the punishment).

There are a lot of people who are motivated by what they don't want. This is a great place to start. It gets people's attention. So when you share stories and experiences in your newsletter be sure to include both the pleasure and the pain, to create a really compelling picture. The goal is to convince your network of the pleasure they will ultimately receive by having a relationship with you, buying your product or your service, and the pain they will avoid by keeping you in their network.

## Getting To Third Base

Now that you have them at second base, you have to help them move on to third base, which turns them into a client. Remember, I don't use my newsletter to get sales, but I do announce free seminars, workshops and events around town. Once your database gets to a certain size, you can negotiate complimentary tickets to different events, and offer them to your subscribers. This is a bonus just for them knowing you.

When I want to make a sale, I do a round-up. I invite my network and their friends to a free value-based event, having announced it at least two to three times in advance (which appeals to multiple convincers). For your Pleasure and Pain Motivators, explain what you will share to eliminate the pain and enhance the pleasure in their lives. And amazingly enough, they show up. They show up because they want to be convinced. Now all you have to do is close the sale. Congratulations! You have done the work to move them to third base.

What happens all too often at this point is that people just stop following up once the sale has been made. You spent all this time and effort creating a client, why would you stop? They have transacted business with you, and there is a potential for future business. Don't let it go to waste. Keep them in the loop. Enroll and engage them. You do this by sending them your newsletter. Otherwise, you will set yourself up to play a losing ball game.

> Most people stop when they get to third base—the sale. Don't stop there!

Think about it. You get to first base, second base, third base and then stop. Then you have to start all over again. If you just keep running the bases, sure, there's lots of activity and busy-ness happening. You're making the sales, but it's a lot of work. You could make more money with less effort. Use the momentum of the sale to move them all the way to home base. If they like your work, and they like you, why wouldn't they want to stay in touch? Keeping in touch by using a newsletter is not that much more work, and the results will pay off again and again. Keep in touch by sending them your newsletter and you can move them forward until you get a home run. Don't stop short of a home run. Go all the way!

## Hitting A Home Run

In order to make a home run, you have to take that client and turn them into an evangelist. An evangelist is someone who brings the sales to you—so you don't even have to move off home plate once you get there. They are the pinch runners that do all of the work running the bases for you, while you sit back and receive all of the benefit. Doesn't that sound like a great idea? Your clients will be the ones generating new business, without you having to do all of the legwork.

### Creating Evangelists

So, how do you create the evangelist? Well, it doesn't happen overnight. It takes time to build credibility and trust in people. You have to be in it for the long haul. It is about being genuine, sincere, and authentic. It is about sharing your core values through the stories in your newsletter, so that you attract the people with whom you share similar values. It is also about showing you care, by taking the time to educate people.

People admire those who are willing to speak to their passion. Evangelists can be suspects, prospects or clients. They are the ones who believe in you. They have engaged with your mission, vision and purpose. For whatever reason, you have inspired them and they love talking about you. You make them feel good about themselves. You are not just someone who sold them something. You empowered them.

Are you passionate about your life? Are you passionate about what you do? Are you committed to helping others? Are you unwavering when faced with challenges? Do you keep your commitments in the face of fear and doubt? Wishy-washy people do not inspire confidence. Only passionate people foster the faith and support of evangelists. Everyone wants someone to believe in, and count on, someone who seems fearless when faced with life's challenges. So take a chance, be passionate and keep your commitments. Be strong when challenged. Have faith. Love yourself and others. Love what you do, and you will naturally create evangelists. Now organize your evangelists and rally the power of their networks into a focused beam.

## Checking Your Response Ratio

This is a very important lesson that I learned from Alex Mandossian. He was speaking at a seminar in California about how he has a database of about 25,000 people. Alex is an internet web traffic conversion specialist. Alex is also one of the top internet marketing gurus in North America and is sought after as a speaker and trainer.

Since 1991, he has generated over $233 million in sales and profits for his clients and partners via "electronic marketing" media, such as TV Infomercials, online catalogs, 24 hour recorded messages, voice/fax broadcasting, tele-seminars, webinars, podcasts and internet marketing.

Alex sent an e-mail out to his database of 25,000 contacts during the morning session. In the afternoon—about 8 hours later, 2,500 of them had responded to the offer. That is pretty good. A 10% response—just over 2,500. That was impressive and I thought if I have to build my database to 25,000 to get that kind of response ratio I really have my work cut out for me. I came back home and shared this with my web guru, who is a Corey Rudl protégé (another internet guru), and he said, "July, you don't have to build a network of 25,000 people to get that kind of response rate, you already have it."

I said, "Excuse me? Are you off of your rocker?"

He explained to me that most people are lucky if they get a response rate of 1–3%. If you get 5–7% that is exceptional. For Alex to get 10% is phenomenal. So that means that Alex is a phenomenal marketer.

And then he said, "Did you know that in your database, over 91% of them open your newsletter within 48 hours of receiving it?" And I thought, "How come only 91% open it? I thought they all opened it."

With a high response rate, your database of 2,500 can equal a database of 25,000.

"July!" he said, "That's unheard of! It's unprecedented. I have never seen stats like this before. They don't normally exist in the industry. Your 2,500 with a 91% response ratio is the equivalent of his net at 10% response. You basically both have the same database potential, you just have a lot higher response ratio. Alex has more people in his database that are not interested, and that's why he has to have a lot higher numbers to draw from."

I think that's cool. I have the response ratio equivalent to having 25,000 people in my database already! My web guru said, that because we know that 91% open my newsletter within 48 hours of it arriving, it shows that people are actually waiting for the newsletter to arrive in their inbox. Now that is the kind of response you want. It means that you are on the right track and that the people in your database are really connected to you. They not only read what you send them, they look forward to seeing what you write about next.

My intent is to educate, inspire and empower people. So I thought about that for a while and wondered, how could I leverage that kind of response rate, and convert it into cash flow. The answer is by having a call to action. Transacting business takes energy. Cash is tied up in your network. It takes energy to free it up to move in your direction. Having a call to action with a value attached, such as free educational seminars, is more compelling than asking people to buy something from you.

When people see a value, the cash flows. That is when I started to think about how far my network reached and how it could enable me to reach an even wider audience—one that was beyond my own database. It became clear to me that time invested in building my network was producing incredible results and with a bit more effort, it could reach even more people.

People share things that they think are valuable. They share advice, tips, and stories. If they liked what I was offering, chances are that they might share it with others in their own network. Reaching out beyond my immediate network, I could see that it was possible to tap into the networks of everyone who was in my network.

# Section Two

## Building Relationships

# Section Two

## Building Relationships

Relationships are the master key to riches. The riches I speak of can be financial success, emotional success, athletic success, spiritual success—you name it. Wherever you see successful people, there are successful relationships that laid the foundation for their success. It is how well we connect and inter-connect with people that determines how successful the outcome.

You see, we are not here on this planet just to accomplish "things." We are here to enrich other people's lives. We are here to express agape—love for all. This is the greatest gift we can impart to others.

Yet that expression of love needs to be active and constant in order to nurture, cultivate and harvest those relationships. For a second, just imagine your relationship with a house plant. At first, when you bring it home from the store, the initial excitement fosters daily care. Then after a while, the watering might become more sporadic. Perhaps you even forget to water the plant altogether. Eventually your plant will die from your lack of attention to its most basic needs.

Relationships are quite similar. You meet someone. There's a connection. You spend time together—on the phone, corresponding, chat at a meeting, go for lunch or dinner. The relationship flourishes. Then the phone calls and correspondence become less frequent. Eventually you lose touch altogether and the relationship dies. You go your separate ways and that's it. Don't let all that energy and time go to waste.

Even if it is not a high priority relationship such as a spouse or significant other, it has inherent value that requires very little effort to maintain. How do you manage a growing network of people on an active and constant basis while maintaining your sanity? You use your newsletter as your stand-in.

Your newsletter does the work of maintaining your business relationships.

In the movie industry, the star is not always on set. The studio hires a stand-in who has the same look and feel of the hero actor. The stand-in fills in for the tedious drudge work so the director can work with blocking and lighting. When all the kinks have been worked out, the hero actor is called on set and takes the place of the stand-in.

Your newsletter is like your stand-in. It does the work of connecting to everyone you meet and know. It saves you the time of writing lots of postcards, letters or e-mails, making phone calls, meeting people for lunch and dinner. These are time consuming and labor intensive activities. Your newsletter can easily take your place by keeping your network up to date on all your events and activities.

When done correctly, your newsletter can turn people on. When done poorly, it can turn people off. If your newsletter turns people on, just imagine their response when you, the hero actor, show up in person or they hear your voice on the phone. Your newsletter has done the work of maintaining your relationships. People will feel special when they get to meet you in person or hear your

## What Does It Cost To Find A New Client?

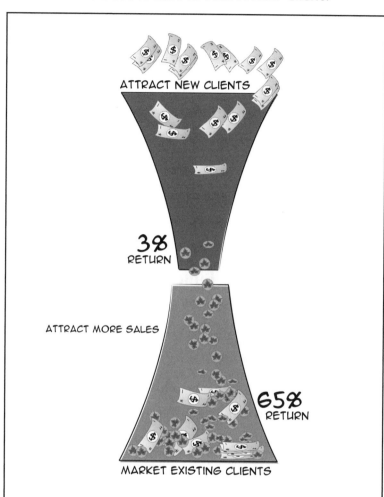

Finding new clients is much more expensive than marketing to your existing clients. You only get about a 3% return for the time and money you put in.

The best return on your investment is in marketing to your existing clients. On average you get an ROI of 65%. Less money put out and a higher return. Now that makes sense.

voice on the phone. And when the time is right, you will then have the opportunity to monetize your relationship. How? It's simple. You will have created so much value just by your stick-to-it-ness, that people will naturally want to work with you. They know you will do what it takes to succeed in spite of any obstacles. They have shared your journey through your newsletter stories.

Most people leave their networking to chance. Successful people have a system to leverage their network. Why leave your success to the winds of fate while your business gets tossed to and fro? Your newsletter is like your motor. It gets you moving by building relationships, while you focus on guiding your business where it needs to go.

## Why Do I Need To Build Relationships?

Building relationships makes life easy. Ignoring relationships makes life hard. Building relationships creates a network of people who feel valued. Ignoring your relationships leaves people feeling like you don't care. Relationships take energy and effort to cultivate. It takes time to build a solid relationship base through your newsletter. It usually takes a year, although there are exceptions to this rule.

It may take a year to build your relationship up with your readers, so be patient.

In my real estate course, one of my students had procrastinated writing her newsletter for eight months. She finally ran out of her own money to invest. So how could she buy real estate with none of her own money? Simple, she would buy it with other people's money. But wait! How could she find joint venture partners who have the money, when she had no system in place for following up? Starting the newsletter now became a priority. She sent out her newsletter and was able to attract a million dollars in

*Take time to cultivate your network. It is filled with very interesting people that you have a real connection with.*

investment money by her third issue. The amazing thing is that she did it without asking for the money. I must mention that this is an exception. Three months is a very quick time frame. In her case, she has a very well established reputation. Her readers responded when she started sharing what was going on in her life. It's that simple. The remarkable thing is that these investors were not people in her immediate circle of influence. They were friends of her friends. That's the power of a newsletter. It can reach more people than just your network.

The thing is, get started now. It doesn't have to be perfect, in fact it's better if it isn't perfect. People will be able to relate to you better if they see you as slightly imperfect and willing to still keep on moving forward. It shows a openness to growing.

## The Value Of Cultivating Your Network

A truly effective network is cultivated through your warm market—people you meet and greet in face-to-face encounters. It seems almost ludicrous when you think about using traditional advertising. Huge dollars are spent on a small ad that is distributed to thousands, hundreds of thousands, millions of addresses, on the chance that your ad will appeal to some stranger who is motivated enough and takes the initiative to contact you. It's a shotgun approach to marketing. That's why this type of advertising usually only generate a 1% to 3% response ratio. And that's not actual sales. The people that respond are still prospects at this point.

Most businesses do not realize that their advertising budgets are backwards. If you advertise to the 100% of your clients who have already done business with you or know you, it will generate 65% more business. You will also come to realize that your continuity program has a lifetime impact. I ask you, what is the lifetime value of connecting to people? To me it's priceless.

> Advertising generates, on average, a 1-3 % response ratio.

Let's face it. People have short term memories. There is so much happening in our lives these days, we are in constant overwhelm and overload. Our brains can only hold the most relevant bits of information. How many times have you been in a conversation where you say or they say, "I'll get you the name of that person," and you end up not following up because it means you would have to call a friend in order to get the information. If you promise it, make sure you follow through. If you don't, others may hear of it through word of mouth.

Word of mouth is by far the most powerful form of marketing. The editor of this book, Cathrine Levan from KickStart Communications, was selected because of an author's raving reviews about her. That definitely caught my ear and my undivided attention. I had been planning to write this book for a few years. In 2005, I began actively sourcing out editors through referrals and surfing the internet. I had found KickStart Communications on the internet a year before and printed off the contact page, but the page sat on my desk for a year. Why? Because I didn't know her and there is no deep connection with just a web page.

In March 2007, I met Jan Addams of Image To Interior Inc. for the second time. She is the author of a great new book called, *Discovering Your Inner Style: 8 Steps to G.U.R.U.* She was in the process of writing a book a year ago and now had the finished product in her hands. When I asked Jan who that person was, I was surprised to hear that she had hired Cathrine Levan of KickStart Communications. This is the very company I had researched the previous year, and Jan was thrilled with her work. I vowed to contact her that day.

Creating a book is just a result. My desire was to have the process of book writing be an enjoyable one. Cathrine has been a delight to work with and I'm looking forward to writing my next book with her. Such is the power and influence of an evangelist.

My first encounter with Jill Lublin was in 2003. She spoke at a business conference about *Guerrilla Publicity*. And I've been bumping into her practically every year since then, at various events where she has either been a keynote speaker or one of the attendees. In 2008, we connected again at the eWomen Network Conference in Dallas, Texas. While sitting together at lunch, she asked if there was anything she could do to help. And bingo! The light went off. I had been asking other established authors if they would like to contribute a Foreword for my book. I completely forgot that Jill was an author too. In my mind, she was a publicist first and an author second. When I asked Jill if she would write a foreword for my book, her response was an enthusiastic yes!

It is a great honor and privilege to have such wonderful people in my network. The point is, that you too can build a network filled with amazing and talented people, by following the steps in Section Four.

You can build a network filled with amazing and talented people.

Once you build a network of amazing people, make it easy for them to refer you around. They will want to help out. They just don't want to be too inconvenienced. Make it easy for them to forward your newsletter with the articles you wrote. That person will in turn, forward your newsletter to their friends. And so on and so on. Make sure your name and contact information appears on every newsletter. Don't make them look for it.

Take good care of your database. Did you know that it is now considered a tangible business asset? It makes good sense to start working on yours sooner rather than later. You may not realize it but you are building equity in your business at the same time as you are making connections with amazing people.

Remember the real estate investor with the million dollars of joint venture money? She has become a money magnet. Instead of chasing after money, money now chases her. It works for other types of businesses as well such as a mortgage broker I met a few years ago. Here is her story.

We met at a seminar. She had just become licensed, and her lamentation was that she could not find business. She had just finished university. She didn't know anyone in her age bracket that was buying real estate and she was broke. How could she start making money? I asked her if she had a continuity program and you can probably already guess what her answer was.

After training with me, she was extremely motivated and created her first newsletter that same month. Her focus was educating people about what to watch out for with different types of mortgages. She then started offering coupons and discounts at some of her favorite restaurants.

A few months later, my husband was talking to her, and she shared with him that over 75% of her business now came from her newsletter. She was so busy from all the business generated by her newsletter, that a year later she sold part of her business. Her database and her newsletter had given her a superior advantage over any other mortgage broker, because she created value for her database, and was able to monetize it.

# 3 Degrees Of Separation

The interesting thing about that story is, the mortgage broker rarely did business with the people who received her newsletter. Her business came from the friends of her network, and the friends of those friends. It's important to understand that your newsletter taps in much deeper than just one level of your network. If you think that you don't know enough people to have a large enough effect, you are wrong. Actually, all you need is to tap into three levels of networks or as I call it, three degrees of separation. Let me explain how the magic works.

Let's say that the average person knows about 200 people, give or take a few. Some people may know 20 people. Others may know 2,000. Whatever your number, you will soon see and understand the miracle of leveraging your

## The 3 Degrees of Separation

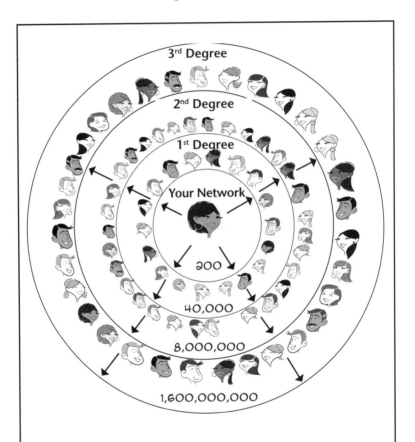

3rd Degree

2nd Degree

1st Degree

Your Network

200

40,000

8,000,000

1,600,000,000

*With a network of only 200 people, you have the potential of reaching over 1.6 billion people. By reaching out to someone in your network, who then reaches out to someone in their network, who then reaches out to a friend in their network, you can extend your influence.*

network. Your network includes family, friends, relatives, neighbors, teachers, doctors, dentists, bus drivers, bank tellers accountants. . . and so on. If you don't think you know very many people, start by making out a list and go from there.

Most people know at least 200 people. Some of you will know more than 200 and some less. For our purposes, we will use an average of 200 people per person. Your immediate "circle of influence" is composed of the 200 people closest to you. They are the core group that you will focus most of your efforts on. Take really good care of them. Shower them in value and do whatever you can to help them with whatever issues they have in their lives.

Let's say that those 200 people know 200 people. That is the first degree of separation; the friends of your immediate friends—people who know your immediate core of people. And that equals 40,000 (forty thousand) people in just the first degree of separation. Now that's a lot of people!

If I say something that has made a positive impact on you, it's likely that you are going to be talking about me to your friends, just in the natural course of your life. And your 200 people will think, "Oh cool," and one of them is going to think, "Wow, I have been searching for something like that for a long time," and that is how it starts coming back to you.

> You don't have to know a lot of people to be successful.

So, that second degree of separation—that friend of your friend—will also know 200 people. That's 40,000 in the first degree of separation multiplied by 200 of their close friends—or 8,000,000 (eight million) people.

Take the 8,000,000 in the second degree of separation and multiply it by 200 of their close friends, and you have 1,600,000,000 (1.6 billion) people in the third degree of separation. That's one-quarter of the population of the planet. This is serious networking. And it also means that you don't have to know 1,600,000,000 people to be successful. You just have to be connected to them so that they can connect with you.

When I tallied up the fourth degree of separation, my calculator went to ERROR. This is actually 320 billion people—more people than are currently on the planet. It's amazing to think that your little group of 200 can reach out to literally everyone on the planet.

So, that is all you need; level one, level two, level three and you are done. At that point you basically have access to everyone in the whole wide world.

When I got this concept, it was a very big Aha! What am I doing trying to grow my database to an enormous size? I am already there. If I just take care of the people I have right now in my network, I can reach virtually everyone on the planet.

**Your immediate "Circle of Influence" averages 200 people**
1st Degree of Separation are the friends of your friends.
200 people x 200 = 40,000

2nd Degree of Separation are the friends of those friends.
40,000 people x 200 = 8,000,000

3rd Degree of Separation are the friends of those friends.
8,000,000 people x 200 = 1,600,000,000

4th Degree of Separation exceeds the population of the planet
1,6000,000,000 people x 200 = ERROR on my calculator

Quite literally, there's someone you know who knows someone, who knows someone, who knows someone, you're connected to 1.6 billion people. It's really a small world with a large number of people in it. Test this out the next time you go out somewhere new. See if you can find someone who knows someone, who you know. It is really quite a fascinating test. Just remember, your reputation will precede you so be sure you cultivate an impeccable reputation and back it up by living up to it.

## Set A Goal

When you start out, you may have only a small following. Over time your database will grow as your friends share your newsletter with their friends. This is the power of the three degrees of separation. Like the commercial says, I shared it with two friends, who shared it with two friends and so on, and so on, and so on.

If you keep a record of how many people you have in your database, you can watch it grow over the first few months. Set a goal to double this number by a specific date. Write this goal down on paper. Then develop a plan on how you will accomplish your goal. This will require you to get out to networking events and talk to people. If you're not getting out at all, then choose to go out once a month. If you're already going out once a week, then bump that up to twice a week. Now you have a strategy and a plan with a purpose.

It's surprising that a lot of people who are growing their business or are just starting a new business don't have a continuity program. Cultivating and expanding your database through the use of your continuity program is an excellent marketing strategy. It will increase your exposure, business opportunities and your net worth.

# Section Three

## Do I Really Need A Newsletter?

# Section Three

## Do I Really Need A Newsletter?

Yes! Absolutely! Unequivocally Yes! If you'd like to be successful and be able to make more money with less effort, then a newsletter is essential. A newsletter will help any business, especially new businesses, grow.

The mistake most people make is they say they'll start a newsletter after the business gets started. Then they'll have something to write about. What a missed opportunity! It's when you are dreaming of the idea of the business, planning it, implementing it, sharing the birth of your business through all its trials and tribulations with your network—this is what creates connection, empathy, understanding, admiration and gets people's attention.

By the time your business is ready for its grand opening, your network has been sharing with their network all about your adventures. Your network will be primed and ready when you launch. It is absolutely crucial. Would you like 75% more business? Or how about a six figure business in one year, without using traditional media advertising?

I will admit that starting a newsletter for the first time was a little intimidating. I had thoughts like, "What would people think? Would they like it? Would they hate it? Will they get annoyed?" I suffered from "other-people-itis." What would other people think of me? Guess what? It didn't matter. What really matters is what you think of yourself. And if someone you know doesn't like staying in touch with you, they really aren't your friend. Why surround yourself with people who pull you down? Surround yourself with people who congratulate you, give praise, encouragement, and admire you for taking action. These are your true friends, the ones that want to see you succeed.

The next biggie that went through my head was the big C word: commitment. I thought, "Once I start, I am committed from this point on." This is a great place to get stuck. You could procrastinate forever. The answer is, just do one newsletter. This newsletter. Today. Tomorrow's newsletter is not here. Just do it one month at a time, month after month. It gets much easier once you take the first step.

Meeting someone once or twice isn't enough time to develop a strong relationship and trust.

The reason that I started my first newsletter was because I knew very few people—about 20 in total. My circle of influence was quite small. At that time, I was a secretary for the municipal sanitation department. I wanted to move ahead but networking at seminars and workshops was not getting me any results. It dawned on me that meeting someone once or twice wasn't enough time to develop a strong relationship. I needed a way to stay in continuous contact with the people I met. How could I develop trust if I only saw them occasionally? The two key components for getting noticed are *time* and *repetition*. There had to be a way to keep me top of mind and yet not have to be everywhere at once. Then it occurred to me. A newsletter is a great way to fulfill the repetition factor without you having to be going in all directions at once.

## Will This Really Work?

People have been reading my newsletter since 2003. Back then I was broke, just starting out in real estate investing and struggling. I was going to a ton of seminars, and let me tell you, that is a lot of work. Eventually the first deal came along. Hey, I got my first building! I would talk about that in my newsletter, and I would recommend courses and books for people to take and read. Then I started getting offers to attend events and seminars. They would say, "July, I can get you in for free."

"Great," I would say. And I would take the tickets and go for free. It was a great perk just for keeping in touch via a newsletter.

> It is amazing how many people will offer free perks for you and your network.

Then, when my database grew larger, I was asked to invite my entire database to attend the events for free. That is when things got really exciting. What a thrill, not to have to pay retail at the consumer desk. I was now a "person of interest" with privileges.

When you have 200 people in your database, people start to look at that. "Hey, July you are more than welcome to invite your entire database to our event. So I would send the newsletters out, and people were so grateful.

I would hear back from them all the time, "Thank you for that seminar, July." It was great to be able to offer free events, valued anywhere from $39 to $1,295 to my entire network. All of a sudden there is more value. More value than you had before you started building your database. Connected people are known as Connectors. Their most valuable resource is their network and their networking skills. They know people, and people know them. You've got to get in the people zone because we're all connected. Ultimately, it's people who transact business. Entities, corporations, institutions and businesses are all run by people. Remember, we are no more than three people away from connecting to over a billion people.

## Expanding Your Comfort Zone

We all have a comfort zone. Biologically we are hard-wired to play it safe. This is due to the fact that there is something in our brain called the Reticular Activation System (RAS for short). To paraphrase, the RAS is comprised of two parts: the reptilian and the mammalian. The reptilian part of the RAS is responsible for physical safety. You have physical reflexes that react instantly to protect you in an emergency without any conscious effort on your part. The mammalian part of the RAS is responsible for emotional safety. When you are under emotional stress the mammalian brain leads you to act in certain ways—flock or freeze, which is why environment is stronger than will power. It drives us to act in ways that it thinks will protect us.

Now, if you are trying to create wealth in your life, this is an important thing to be aware of. Let's say you are broke and surrounded by people who are also broke, you will feel safe because you are in your comfort zone. You will naturally avoid associating with affluent people because it makes you feel uncomfortable. But if you want to become more affluent, hanging around with wealthy people is exactly what you need to do. How do you get over feeling so uncomfortable? Once you become aware of how your brain reacts to keep you safe, you can consciously override your RAS. By making

> Your brain will go into sleep mode if you have a very stressful experience.

*The reptilian part of the RAS is responsible for physical safety.*
*Fight or flight, resist or run away.*

a conscious choice to change, energy starts to flow to your prefontal cortex—a place in the brain which allows you to make new choices in spite of past experiences. This allows you to override your instinctual reactions, and starts you on a new path.

At first it will feel unsafe to step out of your comfort zone and associate with people who are affluent. In order to overcome the influence of your RAS, focus on the people who have "done it." In essence, what you must do is create a new "flock," one that is filled with affluent and dynamic people. They will become your new comfort zone.

Once you are fully established in your new comfort zone, you can go back to your old flock and try bringing them into your new flock, one at a time. You may find that your old friends aren't comfortable with your new affluent mindset. Some of them will make the leap and embrace

## Flock or Freeze?

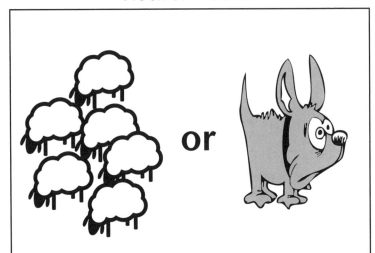

*The mammalian part of the RAS is responsible for emotional safety. When under emotional stress, the mammalian brain tends to flock or freeze, which is why environment is stronger than will power.*

your new flock and others will not. That is the beauty of free will. We can make the choice to take a risk and grow or we can choose to stay the same. If your old flock can't or won't make the leap, they will ultimately hold you back. So stop hanging onto them and allow them to choose their own comfort level. This is all a part of our natural evolution. We can't, and shouldn't force people to follow our path. They have to choose it willingly.

Okay, now remember that the RAS is designed to keep you safe at all costs. If you want to come out of your comfort zone and take a risk, expect to experience a fair amount of resistance. The RAS is so strong that if you have a very traumatic or stressful experience your RAS can actually put you to sleep to protect you. It's a survival mechanism and it serves us well when we are in a traumatic situation.

When we are faced with new experiences, our brain sees them as either a threat or an opportunity. Each new event is either a life threatening situation or an experience that will feed us in some way. At the most primal core, it's all about "eat or be eaten." Survival is the most fundamental human need and our drive to survive will do anything, including knocking us out cold, to keep us from being eaten.

In today's modern era, threats are not so much about sabre-toothed tigers hunting us for food. We deal more with rush hour traffic, computer glitches, never ending e-mails in our inbox, multi-tasking, information overload and constant demands on our time. It still may feel like we're being eaten alive at times, but primarily in this day and age, it is more mammalian threats—emotional safety. The RAS still kicks in, and shuts us down to keep us safe. This explains why we feel very sluggish and tired after a long day of emotional and mental struggles. This is because we don't always have the ability to burn off the stress hormones by running away or fighting.

> Choose to act in spite of fear, doubt, indecision or inconvenience.

The difference with successful people is how they manage their Reticular Activation System. Awareness is the first key. Know that you have it and that you need to manage it.

How do you manage your RAS? Well, one way is to keep expanding your comfort zone so that change is less threatening. So how do you expand your comfort zone? Choose to act in spite of fear, in spite of doubt, in spite of indecision, in spite of inconvenience. You can see as plain as day that writing a newsletter is not life threatening. It won't kill you to write it. Then ask yourself, "What if?" Ask yourself a whole series of "what if" questions. What if you really do make a difference in people's lives? What if you do add value to other people's lives? What if? You really won't

*Choose to act in spite of fear, in spite of doubt, in spite of indecision, in spite of inconvenience. The rewards are worth it!*

know until you do it. Everything else is only speculation, make believe, false evidence appearing real. You are greater than the sum of your biological parts. The more you practice expanding your comfort zone, the easier it gets to soothe the savage beast. Soon you will have that reptile running towards the fear and the mammal purring in contentment. So choose to act in spite of fear and doubt. You can never truly tame the RAS, but you can train it.

You have to start somewhere, why not right here, right now, Today! For me, jumping out of my comfort zone was to start associating with successful people. In the beginning, you can start off by meeting people who are similar to you in net worth, salary, type of car and lifestyle, because this is already within your comfort zone.

It is natural to attract and be attracted to the same energy. I am referring to both external and internal energy, like the external energy you expend as you get out there and start mingling and networking. Or the internal energy of your thoughts and desires focused into a fixated purpose to expand and grow. As your energy increases, the type of people you meet starts to change—you will attract people who are slightly more successful than you, and have larger networks. If you expand your comfort zone just a bit more, you will start meeting millionaires and multi-millionaires. It's a progressive journey. The amazing thing is that as your energy and your network expands, you will notice that your net worth expands in direct response.

Writing your newsletter is also an energy expanding activity. Your self-confidence increases, your writing skills become even more fine-tuned and you will be more sensitive to the energy around you. It will expand your awareness in a way that starts to attract abundance to you. You will start making more money and people will really start to take notice of you. As your network grows, your ability to create good things in your life also grows. With all these amazing benefits, can you see why I want you to get started right away?

## Grow Your Money Blueprint

One challenge with expanding your comfort zone is the money blueprint issue. In 2003, I had a poor money blueprint, I was $40,000 in debt and living with my parents in their basement suite. Why was I broke? I believe that it was because I was financially illiterate. I felt intimidated by rich people because even though the words they spoke were in English, it was like they were talking in Greek or code.

I needed to understand the language of money. In order to do that I had to go right back to the beginning and re-educate myself about money. There is no shame in that. We all have a starting point. If anything, the shame is never starting at all. And rich people get excited when they see someone growing. It is a natural desire to help, nurture, and guide. It's a team effort, because no one becomes successful on their own. They all had help along the way.

So, turn your fear into excitement. Turn anxiety into anticipation, and threat into an opportunity. Reframe your thoughts from I can't, to I can do it. Affirm to yourself, "I don't know," ask "what if" questions and go forward from there.

You may have heard the axiom "Every master was once a disaster." Mastery is a four step learning process. We begin at step one where we all start with Unconscious Incompetence. We are not aware of what we don't know and we don't know how to do it. In step two we become aware of something. We begin to study and learn. This is Conscious Incompetence. We may know what to do, and we're not very good at doing it. In step three we continue to evolve, and with practice we become an expert. This is Conscious Competence. We know what we're doing and we do it well. When we reach step four, we have achieved Mastery. Now we can do it without thinking. This is called Unconscious Competence.

> We all have to start somewhere. Never be ashamed of starting at the beginning.

Remember when you first learned to drive a car, especially a stick shift? Two feet and three pedals: accelerator, brake and clutch. At first it seemed overwhelming. How could you remember which pedal to work, shift, clutch, steer and still focus on a road filled with other drivers at the same time? Eventually you learned how to shift, drive, change lanes and drink coffee while tuning the radio to your favorite station.

We all go through the same learning process, and it's natural to be overwhelmed at first. Just relax, you will adjust in time. People are people. We all have emotional reactions to things so don't worry. Being afraid is normal. Relax into the change and your fear will suddenly shift to excitement.

> Relax into the change and your fear will suddenly shift to excitement.

Back to my journey into financial literacy. I attended seminars and workshops, read all kinds of books and started asking lots of questions. I began to learn the language of money and become financially literate. My vocabulary and comprehension increased over time and my understanding and abilities expanded.

This is where you need to start. It is where everyone starts. Begin with your story, share what you know and it will help others. This will give you purpose and a desire to meet and engage people at networking events. It may start out as your story but it's not about you, it will end up inspiring others who are also starting out on a new path.

Make it your goal to meet one new person every time you go out. That's an easy goal to accomplish. If you start out small, then it's easier to double your goal and decide to meet two new people the next time. Celebrate when you achieve your goal. Mini-celebrations are absolutely necessary to help you stay motivated. After all, it is not easy to step outside of your comfort zone. Remember that each step you take is one that will bring you closer to your million dollar network.

## Networking With A Purpose

Today's business world is full of empty and broken promises. Because of this, I recently stopped giving out my business card. Only 1 out of 20 people would ever follow-up with me, so what was the point of handing out business cards if they were not going to follow-up? Take their card, at least you know that you will follow-up with them. If someone is really persistent in getting my contact information, there is always a pen and paper somewhere.

When you do take someone's business card, assure them that you will follow-up with them by e-mail and that you will send them a copy of your latest newsletter. If you made a connection with this person, they will look forward to receiving it and finding out more about you. Be considerate of people and their time.

> When you say you will do something, then do it, and do it well.

I will admit it right here and now that I am a card collector. The cards that I collect all end up in a shoe box right after they have been entered into my database. I keep them because I have an ironclad rule about following up. People call me a follow-up fanatic, and I am a fanatic with regards to the 24 hour follow-up rule. Always, always, follow-up within 24 hours. There are exceptions to the rule, like when traveling, if you do not have access to your database. In all cases, the information on a business card is entered and then followed up by a personal e-mail greeting. Hey, when you say you are going to do something, then do it well, and do it in a timely manner. This will impress people, including yourself.

When you start networking don't go after just anybody. Look for that special person. You know the one. There's a special connection, when your eyes meet or when you shake hands. They are easy to talk to and there is instant rapport. When you find that person, you will want to stay in touch with them. They are diamonds in the rough just waiting to be polished into genuine relationships through time and repetition. Remember that time and repetition can turn suspects into prospects.

There is an important distinction between prospecting and networking. Tim Sanders, author of *Love is the Killer App*, wrote an excellent article in the December 2008 issue of *Success* magazine, where he states that too often people mistake prospecting and brokering for networking. Looking for customers with business cards in hand is not networking. Taking a commission for connecting two people is not networking. True networking is a gift you give to others. So stop brokering and focus on networking.

When you meet someone and you are exchanging business cards for the first time, remember to:

- Tell them you'll follow-up
- Tell them you're including your newsletter
- Follow-up

In your follow-up e-mail, you can include the following:

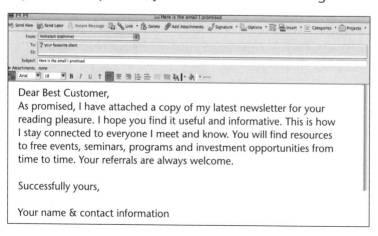

Dear Best Customer,
As promised, I have attached a copy of my latest newsletter for your reading pleasure. I hope you find it useful and informative. This is how I stay connected to everyone I meet and know. You will find resources to free events, seminars, programs and investment opportunities from time to time. Your referrals are always welcome.

Successfully yours,

Your name & contact information

This conveys to them that you are a person who keeps promises and begins the process of building trust.

Be a refreshing change, a promise of hope, and stay at their top-of-mind by following up promptly. You will then have separated yourself from the masses. This gives you an unconscious priority in that person's mind over someone else who is consistently tardy or who simply doesn't show up and Bingo! You have instant credibility. You have already racked up points right out of the gate. What a great first impression. Now make a great lasting impression.

You asked for permission to send them the first newsletter when you followed up, right? If you still feel a little uncomfortable putting them on the list, you could send a more formal invitation by asking them to opt into a permission-based subscription when you send them the first e-mail.

## Asking For Help

In the beginning, your newsletter will require some testing and tweaking. Thankfully you will be able to circumvent the trials and tribulations that I went through. I did some big no-nos and learned from those lessons. I may not have all the answers but I do know this, other people will have answers to my questions and I have answers to other people's questions.

Collectively, as a whole, we are geniuses. Why work alone when you can tap into the genius of the whole? So think of building your network like you are gaining more brain cells with each contact you add. You may not personally, have the answer to a particular problem, but someone in your network probably does. This is the true power of a network. Don't be scared to tap into it. It is a fantastic resource, one that will become a constant source of amazement and wonder the more you use it. And of course, the great part about having a network is that the more you use your network the stronger it gets. It is part of our nature to want to help others. So don't be shy, give your network the opportunity to help you when you need it.

This brings up another comfort zone issue: asking for help. Even the Lone Ranger had Tonto to depend on. If you are too young to remember, the Lone Ranger was a weekly television show. This good samaritan cowboy would dress up in a mask and ride around the country on a horse to free the good people from the oppression of the bad guys. Tonto was his sidekick partner who always came to his rescue when things didn't turn out so well.

We are not designed to work alone, so make sure you ask for help.

As humans we are not designed to work alone. We are designed to live and work in tribes. We live and work in communities with lots of other tribes. And there are a lot of resources that you can tap into. People are willing and able to help because we are, by nature, caring and helpful. Our biological imperative is to survive, and we do so, in tribes. Learn to ask for help. It is as simple as saying, "Please help me" or "Can you help me?" or "Do you know anyone who can help me?"

There is always someone in your network who will be able to help. If not, they may know someone from their network who can. Asking for help isn't being weak. It's demonstrating that you have the strength and confidence to allow others to help you. It also allows others to feel that their gifts are being accepted and valued. We all like to contribute, so let others contribute by giving back to you. It's a real win-win.

## The Purpose Of The Page

The true purpose of the page is to inspire others. It's not about sales or about having a loyal following. It's about sharing your journey with other like-minded people. You will never really understand how valuable your newsletter is until you hear how it has touched someone's life. We all like to hear how others make it through tough times, and when we share our good times and bad, it helps others.

Your failures, your challenges and your dilemmas are just as important to share as your successes. How did you deal with the rough time last year when the market dropped? What did you do to overcome it? Making it through tough times demonstrates character. Life can get turbulent at times. It's how you deal with it that matters. A positive attitude is the key to a great newsletter.

You will be amazed at the responses you get when you are vulnerable. It really hits a chord with people. Some of the e-mails that I receive say, "Thanks for sharing July. That story came just at the right time." It's very fulfilling.

All of our experiences are common experiences. We think that we are the only ones going through them but we are not. You never really know what people are going through until you share your stories with them.

> My newsletter gave her a sense of hope when times were tough.

This brings to mind the story of a woman who saw me speak at a seminar. She felt inspired by my story and signed up for my newsletter. I never heard from her again. Two years later, a beautiful two page letter arrived from her, thanking me for sending her my newsletters. As I read the letter my eyes filled with tears. She wrote, "I read your newsletters every month and it gave me hope to keep going and not give up. You have been through a lot of very tough times yourself, and sharing your stories with me really helped. I can't stop now because I just tell myself, 'If July can do it, I can do it too.'"

She now has a successful and thriving business. Many times she felt like giving up, and then my newsletter would arrive. It inspired her to keep on moving forward in spite of all the obstacles in her path. I suddenly realized that my newsletter had changed the course of her life. That was when the monumental impact of my newsletter really hit home. My writing was giving someone a sense of hope. That day my newsletter became more than just a newsletter. It became part of my mission, vision and purpose in this life—to inspire and empower the world to live in hope and victory in order to create a global community based on contribution and cooperation. I am now fulfilling that mission with my newsletter and all I can say is Wow! What a great feeling it is to know that you are touching people's lives with something as simple as a newsletter.

> I am fulfilling a mission with my newsletter and all I can say is Wow!

Whose life will your newsletter touch? What is the world missing if you hold yourself back? You bring a little bit of brilliance to this universe every time you expand your comfort zone, so let your light shine.

There are times that you will fall on your face and have to pick yourself up. One of the gifts of having your network is that you can offer encouragement to them, and other times you will receive it from them. At some moment in our life everyone needs support. If you are connected to a network of amazing people, they will be there for you just like you are there for them.

## Reframing Your Reactions

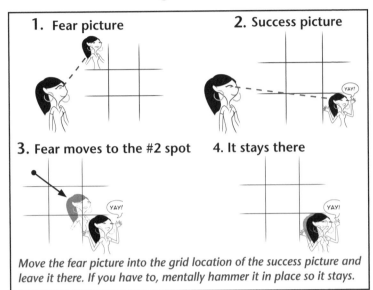

Move the fear picture into the grid location of the success picture and leave it there. If you have to, mentally hammer it in place so it stays.

There is one other strategy to help you overcome your resistance to starting your newsletter. It's a strategy for reframing your bad picture into a good picture. Believe it or not, we all see in pictures. For example, when I tell you not to think of a "pink elephant," you probably just saw, in your mind's eye, an image of a pink elephant.

In the same way, when I ask you to not to think about your fear of writing a newsletter, what do you see? You immediately think of your fear of writing. So let's do a little experiment. If you were to place your fear of writing on a tic-tac-toe grid, where would the picture be located?

Imagine a tic-tac-toe grid is hanging in space in front of you. Vertically: Is your fear near the top, near the center or near the bottom? Horizontally: Is it to the left, center or right? Mark that as Spot #1. Do you smell popcorn?

Now I'm going to ask you to think about one of your most successful experiences. It was a glorious day and you felt like a champion. Go ahead. Do that fist pump and shout, "Hoorah!" You are anchoring in that powerfully positive experience.

Next, think of the tic-tac-toe grid hanging in space in front of you. Vertically: Is your Hoorah! picture near the top, near the center or near the bottom? Horizontally: Is it to the left, center or right? Mark that as Spot #2.

Hey, do you smell popcorn? . . . There, did you just feel a momentary blip in your brain? Did you ask, "What the heck does popcorn have to do with anything?" That was a quick state change. The question was designed to stop you from whatever you were doing, and give you a fresh clean slate. It's almost like pushing a reset button in your brain.

> Reframe your fear so that it is no longer the most powerful driving force in your life.

Now go back to the first picture. The not so great, I'm scared of writing picture. The fear picture. You left it in Spot #1. Now move it to the Spot #2 position and leave it there. Your brain hard-wired your success pictures into Spot #2. Moving your fear picture into Spot #2 automatically neutralizes your fear. You are reframed.

Every person's brain has their own unique spot on the grid for their fear picture and success picture. Know that your reframe will not match everyone else's. Once you have moved your fear picture so that it lives in your success spot, that's it. You're done! You have just reframed your fear and told your brain that fear is not the most important feeling.

If your picture doesn't move easily or keeps snapping back, then imagine a construction team with strong chains and hooks to haul it to Spot #2. Then take a hydraulic hammer and nail it down so that it stays in place.

This exercise reframes your fear so that it is no longer the most powerful driving force in your life. Since fear and success can't exist in the same space, the fear has to go. That's not to say that you will completely lose your fear of writing in one reframe session. It's that your fear of writing has now lost its seat of power. It no longer controls you. You can wait an hour or wait a day, and when you go back to your writing, you will find that it comes much easier from now on.

## The Power Of The Page

I met Jerry, a property manager, at a seminar in Alberta where he was one of the keynote speakers. It was a really good seminar and I enjoyed his message so I introduced myself to him and we had a two minute conversation. I told him about my newsletter and said that I would follow-up by sending it to him. I went back home and e-mailed him and said, "Thanks for sharing, you were fantastic and I learned a lot. As promised, here is a copy of my newsletter and I just want to stay in touch with you." That was early in spring. Six months went by and he had received about six issues of my newsletter.

In September, I was going back to Alberta and wondered, who I knew there that I could network with? Oh yeah, Jerry lives there. So I called him up and said, "Hey Jerry, remember me? It's July! We met at your seminar." He kind of remembered me and he kind of knew the name because it's unique. I told him that I was coming to Alberta and would love to take him out for dinner. Was he available? No doubt he was thinking, "Oh my! A girl wants to take me out for a free dinner, sure I'm available." And so I did.

We were sitting across the table enjoying dinner at one of his favorite restaurants and he said, "You know, you seem very familiar to me. We have met somewhere else besides my seminar. I know we have." He started listing off all the seminars he had taken, and as it turned out, we had done a lot of the same seminars but not at the same time. Our dates were not coinciding, so he just let it go, figuring that he would eventually remember.

He started telling me that his biggest challenge as a property manager, was looking for new clients. This didn't make sense to me so I asked him, "Why are you working so hard Jerry? You are so good at what you do, and you have your business all systemized. How come people aren't banging down the doors to get you to handle their properties?" He told me that he didn't know why. He said that he had to get out there and find all of his clients himself. I asked him, "Why is that? You already have happy customers. Don't you have a continuity program?"

"What is that?" he asked.

"Well, do you have a newsletter?"

"I have been thinking about it," he said.

"What do you mean, you are thinking about it? I send you my newsletter every month." And all of a sudden it was like a light went on in his head.

He pointed his finger at me and blurted out, "I read your newsletter every month."

And I just said, "I know."

"That is where I have seen you," he said. The realization swept through his brain as all the dots began to connect in his head. We really hadn't known each other except from that one seminar. My newsletter was the only connection, yet he felt as if he had known me for years. Every month I came into his inbox regularly and consistently. He saw my face month after month in my newsletter, *July News*. He read about my trials and tribulations, my successes and my challenges.

Over a period of six months, I became solidly imprinted in his subconscious as someone he knew. His memory was telling him that we were in a long standing relationship, but in reality, he knew me because of my newsletter. Wow—I had no idea my newsletter had such an incredible impact on people. While I was busy focusing on business, my newsletter was building a strong foundation with Jerry! The message was drilled into my brain. Newsletters are an incredibly powerful communication tool.

In a way a newsletter is like television advertising—you are always bombarded with the same ads day after day. They get stuck in your head and eventually you find yourself repeating their slogans. Your newsletter acts in the same way. You show up in the comfort of their home or their office in pictures and words. Pretty soon it's like you are a normal part of their life. You become familiar, even if you don't see them or speak to them on a regular basis. It's a simple and effective way to become more memorable.

## What Is Stopping You?

The only thing stopping you is YOU. Fear is fear. When it all comes down to it, excuses are just that, excuses. What will people think of me (Fear)? I can't think of anything to write (Excuse). I don't have enough time (Excuse). I'm too old, I'm too young, my English is not good enough yet, I'm too tired—whatever your excuse is, it's just an excuse. Don't let it trick you into thinking that it is real because it's not.

So what's stopping you? If you were guaranteed a one million dollar inheritance in cash, would you make the effort to go get it? Or would you let fear and excuses get in the way? Let's try out a scenario and see.

You receive a phone call from an executor because a long lost uncle, several times removed, has written you into his last will and testament. You are to receive one million dollars cash. Are you available to come down to the office? Wherever that office is located, I'm sure you will find a way to get there, and quickly. For a million dollars who wouldn't?

You arrive at the stately office of a venerable old law firm. You are given a piece of paper and you read what is on it. The instructions are clearly stated. You have inherited one million dollars cash. The only problem is, the key to the safety deposit box is locked in a chest, buried near the top of Mount Kilimanjaro.

Just as you're thinking of hiring a team of professional mountain climbers to retrieve the chest for you, the lawyer points out that there is a stipulation that requires you to make the climb yourself or you would forfeit the cash. You have the next 365 days to retrieve the key or the inheritance will all go to charity. What would you do?

Think of your newsletter in the same way as you would that million dollar chest buried on the mountain. Your newsletter holds the key to untold treasures when it's unearthed. All you have to do is go and get it. When you choose not to do it, the treasure, that could have been yours, goes to other fortune seekers who are ready and willing to do what it takes.

Here is a true story about Selena, a Chinese immigrant and a would-be real estate investor. I challenged Selena to write a newsletter. She said, "But I don't speak good

English. I don't write good English."

"Oh, my," I said. "What a good excuse! Are you going to let that stop you?"

"But people will make fun of me. They will make fun of my English," she moaned.

"Do they laugh at you now when you speak to them?" I asked.

"No," she replied. At this point she had to decide if she was able to overcome her embarrassment and face her fear.

Be aware that if you are embarrassed or ashamed, it will come across in your writing. But if you are proud of the fact you are an immigrant just learning to speak the language, you will share that pride and excitement with them without even trying. And don't be afraid to share your faults, because people love that.

Your newsletter doesn't need to be perfect. It's more realistic if it isn't.

I said to her, "You don't need to be perfect, because then people will probably think, 'Oh she is so perfect all the time, I don't want to invest with her.' But if you are just yourself, they think, 'Wow, here is a person with all these disadvantages and she is very successful. That is inspiring. She must be a real fighter, I want to invest with her, because she will fight to get the best deals.' So just get out there and do it. Imperfection is okay!"

And Selena said, "Oh, I have never thought about it that way." So she went out and wrote her first draft newsletter. I gave her a 48 hour deadline and she made it. It wasn't a perfect job, because her newsletter wasn't meant to be perfect. I just wanted to see if she could face her fears.

Most people stop right here because they think, "I can't do that. I don't know what to write. What would I say? No one is going to be interested in what I have to say."

All of our standard fears come out. Everyone has to face these fears when they move forward. Most people give up and run away, but Selena didn't run away. She faced her fears and wrote her first newsletter.

> It's all about educating, inspiring, empowering people and giving value.

It was chock-full of typos, grammatical and syntax errors, jumping from thought to thought, unfinished sentences, you name it. That didn't matter. She had a first draft newsletter. It was a start. Now we could make it better, add ideas, remove ones that didn't work and get clear on which stories to share. The typos were the least of our concerns.

All you really have to do is share your story. People are interested in your story—they are not interested in a bunch of facts. It's not that you have to avoid facts, go ahead, throw in a few. The important thing is that you share in a way that is inspiring and empowering to others. Your stories are the meat and potatoes of your newsletter. Make sure they are rich, hearty and full of flavour.

When Selena called me to go over her newsletter, we went through it and fixed up her grammar so that it made more sense to her readers, and she learned. Because this was her first newsletter, people were not going to believe it if it were to show up

> Your newsletter is not about showing off your educational credentials.

too perfect. If it were edited until it was absolutely perfect, it would seem less personal. She needed to build rapport with her audience first, right where she was at, imperfect English and all. It is important that your newsletter matches who you are and your skill level. If it doesn't match, it will come across as fake, or worse, it will seem like a slick marketing ploy. And so I told her that she *must not* make it perfect.

"What will they think?" Selena complained. "I am a university graduate, I should have good English."

"No," I said. "Your newsletter is not about showing off your educational credentials. It's all about being authentic, genuine and real." So she did that. She expressed who she was, and shared some of her struggles to learn English, in an upbeat tone. The grammar was pretty bad, but it was so cute, and now she could proudly say that she had written her first newsletter.

As each issue progressed, we cleaned up the grammar a little bit more each time, until after one year, her skill level was such that we could hand it over to someone else to edit, and no one noticed.

Now, she still writes it, but someone else edits it for her. It had to be done in gradual stages, because being too polished right away would come across as inauthentic or too much like a piece of mass marketing junkmail.

Remember, just be yourself. Be real . . . be seen . . . be heard . . . be shared.

# Section Four

## Getting Started

# Section Four

## How Do I Get Started?

Convinced? I bet you are. And are you ready to take the next step to get that newsletter started? You have some ideas. You have pen and paper. You have a computer, so why aren't you typing? You are probably asking yourself, "What do I do next? I don't know the first thing about how to start writing a newsletter." Well, don't worry. This section is the how-to part: How to create something amazing out of nothing.

The best time to get started is *Right Now!* Start with where you are at today. No, don't wait until after you've got your act together. Don't wait until after you've got the business plan written or have finished your taxes. And don't wait until you have something to show. The time to start is *Right Now.* Why is this important? Your readers need to be able to relate to your beginnings, your dreams, your challenges and your struggles. They need to see your progress from nothing to something. They need to be taken along on your journey. They need to experience you saying you're going to do something and then read about you actually doing it.

Promises are easy to make and much harder to keep. That's why a newsletter is an excellent motivating factor. You have to keep your promises because people are watching. People take notice when you share with them as the results start showing up in your life. When you share your successes your readers get to live those successes, experiencing them vicariously through you. Make sure that you keep sending your newsletter out every month. Be consistent.

Why do I recommend you start a newsletter? Because it's the most effective continuity program around. It's simple, low cost and yet very effective.

## The First Step

Before you take the plunge, you need to get an overview of the concept of writing your newsletter. Your newsletter should tell your story in a casual framework. Its purpose is to keep you front-of-mind to everyone in your network. You've heard the phrase "out of sight, out of mind." What you do not see, you do not remember right away, but it's in the back of your mind somewhere until something triggers it. Why would you want to be relegated to the back of their mind? Be the pro-active trigger that keeps pulling you to the front of their mind. You want your face imprinted in their brain and your stories to be on their lips. In essence, you want to be imprinted on their long term memory, not their short term memory.

Your successful newsletter should consist of:
- Your smiling photograph
- Only one page of writing
- Sent out only once per month
- Offers a perceived value

Your newsletter should never come across as a series of pre-written letters. The best way to keep it fresh is to make sure that only one-third of the content is pre-written,

*You may feel vulnerable when you first start sharing your newsletter. It takes courage to step out and show the world what you are up to. Keep going, it's worth it!*

such as a lesson plan. The remaining two-thirds must be current. It has to reflect your most recent interactions or thoughts with relevant news media. This keeps your newsletter topical and intriguing. Otherwise, it can become dull and dead. If there is something timely and exciting in your newsletter, then your readers will be hanging on your every word, wanting to know the latest. If it is pre-written and not relevant to right now, there is no reason to read it today. They can set it aside and read it some other time. And you know, some other time quickly turns into never.

A quick and easy method of figuring out what to put into your newsletter is the 3-30-300 method. Basically, you write 3 stories in 30 minutes using a total of 300 words. It's an easy formula for getting you over the hurdle of what to write. Follow it and you will find writing your newsletter a breeze. Don't worry, we will go over it in more detail in Section Five.

OK, now as for what type of stories to include, one of your stories can be educational. It should not be about delivering facts and figures. How boring is that? You would lose your audience about as fast as if you were quoting government statistics. The lesson plan (as I call it) is designed to educate and enlighten in order to empower your reader. The key is to *educate to empower* others. Use statistics sparingly. Make sure there is a point for using them. Otherwise, facts and figures will just seem like filler. If you need to inform with a lot of facts and figures, insert a link where readers can find more details if they are interested.

When you are writing, place an invisible value of $100 per word. This is a great technique to keep the use of your words direct and to the point. A rambling newsletter can lose focus and interest. Keep in mind as well, that people are not interested in the features as much as the benefits. Why go off on a tangent talking about this feature and that feature and wasting words when you can focus on the benefits. Benefits are personal, they tell your readers how your information relates to and will help them. Your readers are more focused on how something will solve their problem than on how cool something is. People respond to the emotional benefit. In the end, your final version should be succinct, clear and full of how they can benefit by staying in contact with you.

> When you are writing, place an invisible value of $100 per word to help you be succinct.

I learned a valuable lesson from The Billion Dollar Man, Bob Circosta. He is the creator of the original Home Shopping Channel and has sold over $1,000,000,000 (one billion) worth of product on television. He has a simple and effective formula known as WSGAT: What's So Great About That. He found that people relate to benefits more than features. The more benefits offered, the more value and the more exchange of energy in the form of cash. The key to his sales was not selling. All he did was focus on the benefits and create more value. The sales just naturally came when he did that. So make sure that your newsletter clearly shows the benefits of staying connected to you.

> A digital camera is a very valuable tool, so keep it with you at all times.

One thing to keep in mind is that pictures speak volumes. They give you instant credibility. You might say that you met a "person-of-influence," and people may take your word for it, or they may not. When they see a photo of you with that "person-of-influence," this is undisputed proof that what you are saying is the truth. It goes a long way towards building trust with the people in your network, so always carry a digital camera with you. Digital cameras are also a compact and inexpensive way for you to diarize your activities. It is a very valuable tool, so keep it with you at all times.

When you finally get started sending your newsletter and are consistent every single month, people will start to realize, "Wow, she just keeps showing up. She comes into my inbox every month, it's only one page, and it's an easy read. Let's see what she's been up to this month."

How do I know this? They've told me, "July, you are the only one that I read. Everyone else I delete. You are my five-minute computer break. I am at the office, I'm busy, and then when your newsletter comes into my inbox, I think, 'Oh great, I get to take a little break and see what July is up to,' and I read it right away." They look at my newsletter, take five or seven minutes out of their day and get a little positive boost. I've gotten their attention—even

*Follow a few simple rules and your newsletter will be the one that people won't delete, as soon as it comes in.*

if it's only for five minutes. They say, "There is July again!"

What's important is that just a little thing like that moves you from being "good" to "great." Very few people have the discipline to be consistent. I have mentored lots of people and they usually start and stop. Why would you stop if you want to be any kind of credible business owner? What you will have done by doing that is educate people to think, "Oh yeah, so-and-so will start a newsletter and in six months down the road, they will quit."

So, if you are a quitter, when you go up to people and say, "Hey, I am real estate investor," or "I am doing this business now and I want your money," people will have already been preprogrammed that in six months from now, you will quit. They will think, "If he can't even do a newsletter for any length of time, he's not committed to that business." It's an unconscious reaction—they are not even aware of it on a conscious level. But it taints your business, because how you do anything is how you do most everything. Most often, people live true to their nature. It takes a real conscious effort to change your instinctual patterns, so don't quit. Keep it going no matter what.

And now after writing over 60 issues, I have hit the 5 year mark. People look at the number of issues I have written and think, "Wow, this person is around for the long haul. She is totally committed and consistent." Consistency equals trust.

Trust is a commitment emotion. When trust is earned, people want to give you their money. And they want to give you their friends' money as well.

So I say to people, the money is out there. People who have over $100,000 to invest are not in scarcity mode, they are in wealth-creation mode. They want to create more assets, they want to create more passive income. You must learn to communicate in wealth-creation language. I'm not talking about big words with lots of syllables. I am referring to the language of abundance, choices, solutions, learning, and growing. Let's choose to reframe the everyday everywhere can't-do mantra into a can-do attitude. This is what separates the leaders from the followers.

> Don't be a quitter. That will break trust with your network. Keep it going.

Now that you have your newsletter, share it with everybody. Not just those in your immediate circle of influence—everybody. And I mean absolutely everybody—the whole world. And that is a scary place to go. You're exposing your views. You're vulnerable to criticism. That's why it takes courage to get started. As you share and continue writing, your confidence increases. You soon realize that anyone who chooses to criticize is really talking about themselves, not you. They need to point the finger at someone else instead of acknowledging their own faults.

> Be direct. Don't use words that hedge what you want to say. Just say it!

The words that come out of a person's mouth are a reflection of their inner self. It's not about you. When you stand tall and stand firm, your readers will respect and admire you as a person of courage. That's why they choose to continue reading your newsletter. So, share

*A casual newsletter from "Yours Truly," to your audience creates a deeper connection with people you meet.*

the things that you have accomplished and the struggles you've had along the way. It will help your readers get to know and appreciate who you are, and it may also help someone who is going through a similar struggle.

There are newsletters from almost every industry. There are stock market newsletters, real estate newsletters, mortgage newsletters, network marketing newsletters. Whatever industry you can name, there is a newsletter for that industry. These types of newsletters perform a function which is industry-specific, mainly delivering facts and figures about that industry. They are also essential for maintaining good business relations but the effectiveness of the newsletter generally does not expand out beyond the immediate recipient list.

A casual newsletter from you to your network, creates a deeper connection that is multi-functional. You are freed from the stereotype of whatever industry you represent which tends to be impersonal, and evolves into an all-pervasive personal relationship. And the people in these networks tend to share personal newsletters more frequently than business-related ones.

Think of your dentist. He or she performs dental hygiene to keep your teeth healthy and functional. You think of that person only as a dentist performing dental functions. Think of golf. You meet your dentist at the driving range. It takes a moment for you to realize who that person is. The dentist is out of context with the environment you are used to seeing him or her in. You discover that your dentist has a 10 handicap and teaches golf lessons privately on the side. Perhaps your dentist could teach you how to lower your handicap. You would be surprised at what you will learn about someone when you read their newsletter.

> If you ever choose to leave a profession for another career, your network won't care.

In the context of a casual newsletter, you would now think of the dentist as a person who does dentistry, and teaches golf. They are a multi-dimensional person. In the same way, I wish for you to become a multi-dimensional person to your network. So if you ever choose to leave a profession for another career, your network won't care. They'll be rooting for you, not the business you left.

This is a company's goodwill. In Wikipedia, goodwill is listed as a term used to reflect the portion of the market value of a business entity not directly attributable to its assets or liabilities. In other words, peoples' loyalty is given a dollar value figure. It's a good idea for you to start an active campaign that builds good will. It's added value.

## What Do I Call My Newsletter?

The title of your newsletter is really up to you. My advice would be that whatever you name it, it should relate to you. One of my students, Mia Yu, asked me what she should call her newsletter. She had absolutely no idea. *Mia's Newsletter*, was the best she could come up with. That's not bad for a start. The key is to create an association through your branding. Your newsletter is something that defines you. It's going to stick with you for the rest of your life. So we started a brainstorming session to loosen things up. We played the rhyme game. What rhymes with your name, Mia? Mama-Mia. Mia See-ya. Yu View. We had fun. Not that she was going to use these titles. Brainstorming is designed to free up your creative genius and gets you connected with who you are. Then when you least expect it, your core message will pop out. At the end of our brainstorming session she chose to call her newsletter: *From Mia To Yu.*

## How Many Pages Do I Have To Write?

Keep it simple. One page only. I'll bet that you receive newsletters into your inbox even now. Do you read any that are over two pages long? The answer is probably no. There are people I know who send out five or seven page newsletters. I don't have the time or the brain capacity to go through all their facts and facts and more facts. They don't have any stories, just lots of facts. Don't go there, it's boring. If you absolutely must have a two page newsletter because there simply isn't room for just one page, guess what? Your newsletter will probably get deleted.

When you start to write your newsletter there are certain things that you should and shouldn't do. One of the big no-no's is selling. Your newsletter is not about selling stuff. It is about helping, educating and connecting with people by sharing your experiences. It is about adding value to people's lives, not lining your own pockets. If you put in too many facts or try to sell products, people will start to shut off.

No matter how tempting it is, keep your newsletter to one page, and don't sell anything. If you absolutely need to give more information, then insert a link to your website or blog and the readers who choose to, can get the rest of the story. Play around with the column width and font size to make your ideas fit. However, it is a good idea to keep things consistent from newsletter to newsletter.

The good news for those of you who are feeling writing challenged, is that it's not a lot of words. Three paragraphs are all you need for an effective newsletter. You can use big print and insert pictures. We all think in pictures. When I ask you to think of a horse, do you see a picture of a horse or do you see the letters h-o-r-s-e? You see a picture of a horse, of course. Pictures make a statement. People may not remember the story but they will remember the picture. Pictures give words a visual connection. If you have no pictures to use in an issue, then use an animation or a graphic and that will be just as effective. I'm hoping you get the picture.

*Which do you see in your mind's eye when you think of a horse? Do you visualize the words or the horse?*

We're all human. We experience the same emotions and struggles and triumphs. If I am facing a challenge, then I know other people are too. Share it. Show them how you manage to get out of the tight spots you have gotten yourself into.

Let's face it, life is a roller coaster ride. You have your ups and downs. Telling your story in the newsletter is not about sharing how depressed you are. It's about sharing strategies on getting yourself out of the doldrums. Ask yourself, "What do the successful people do?"

It is challenging to say you've got a great life when it is not so great. Be grateful during the down times. When you look at it, you've got it pretty good. You're reading this book. That means you have the money and the time to read this book. There are millions of people who cannot even read. I am grateful to be able to read and write. What are you grateful for? Ask yourself this question when you're having a bad day. What are you grateful for?

> Ask yourself this question when you're having a bad day. What are you grateful for?

Instead of asking yourself "Why is this happening to me?" ask yourself, "What lesson can I learn from this? How can I receive more value from this lesson?" Then share it with your readers. Your insights may very well help someone in a similar dilemma.

People want to feel that they are being valued for who they are, not for their wallet. Your network stays connected with you because they relate to your values. Make it a mission to educate, inspire, empower and give value to other people. In return, your network will respond to your needs and give back to you.

You will naturally write what you are absolutely passionate about. That's good! Just don't make it a sales-job. Promote your passion instead of trying to convince them to buy.

The next big no-no is starting every sentence with "I" did this or "I" did that. Big deal. Remember, "What's so great about that?" Always think, how does that affect your readers? What's in it for them? Find the value for them, and share it.

People need to relate your story with something in their life. Whenever you write an "I" sentence, then a "You" sentence must follow. We are trained to write in the first person (too subjective) or the third person (too objective). There needs to be a balance between the two forms of writing in order to write a great newsletter. You need to keep it personal, not self-centered. You need to keep it objective, and yet not come across as aloof.

## How Do I Section My Newsletter?

Many people ask me what they should put into their newsletters. That is really up to you! But, a good content mix is about 50% summarizing your month, 30% on what's coming up and 20% educating people on your area of expertise. Or split into thirds: 33% is your personal editorial, 33% is a lesson plan and 33% is a current event. This is a perfect size for Helpful Hints or a Tip-of-the-Month.

*A good ratio for content*

A typical newsletter template is composed of a letter-sized page. There is a header and a footer and two or three columns. Your smiling photograph, or headshot, is placed in the top left corner below the header. The template uses up a lot of space so don't worry about not having enough to say. The rest of the area is for you to fill. We will go over a very easy way to create content on page 105 called the 3—30—300 formula.

Your smiling photograph must always go at the top of the newsletter either in the headline or just beneath it. It can be located to the left, center or right; just be consistent with its location. Your smile is the first thing your subscriber will see when your newsletter loads. A smile begets a smile and your smiling face will set the tone for the newsletter so make sure that it is prominently displayed.

The header contains a title that will become part of your brand. People will begin to associate your newsletter title with you. It's a great idea to use your name in the title to solidify that association. My newsletter is a deliberate play on my name. *July News in December,* is a pattern interrupt. People think of summer and sunshine in a dreary month. It's a playful hit and it works for me. Find what works for you.

The footer contains your contact information and your disclaimer. If you use a third-party online distribution service, the disclaimer is tagged at the bottom below your newsletter instead of in the footer.

Your contact information contains your name, address, phone number and e-mail address. It is advisable to use a Post Office Box for an address and a toll-free number, to protect your identity. It makes good sense to take care.

A good photographer is worth the investment.

As I said before, your headshot is important. It visually expresses your personality and character. I have mine done professionally, by a headshot photographer—not a portrait photographer. A good photographer will have a whole portfolio of headshots. The good ones work mainly in the entertainment industry.

Find a photo style that you like and explain to the photographer what you like about that photograph. These types of photographers charge a sitting fee and afterwards, the photos belong to you. A good photographer is worth the investment. They are able to capture aspects of you on film, that regular photographers will miss entirely.

When you have a good photograph and you have filled in the header and footer data, it will be time to start writing. If writing 12 newsletters sounds like an incredibly daunting task for you, you can always split it up into smaller chunks. Why not write your newsletter every two months, or plan three newsletters spaced out over four months or four newsletters spaced out over three months? At the very least, write one newsletter per year. The important thing is to get started— right now, and I am going to show you how to do it with my foolproof plan.

This is one of the most inexpensive forms of marketing that is available to you. The investment of your time is well worth your effort so gather up your courage and let's get to it.

> At the very least, write one newsletter per year.

In the next section I will walk you through the process of writing your first newsletter. Since there are many different ways to go about it, you may find a certain way that works best for you. That's great! Feel free to customize the process until it fits your writing style, your skills, and your way of doing things.

If you absolutely cannot conceive of writing a newsletter on your own, there are excellent resources available on Elance.com or CraigsList.org. Just search for freelance writers. Dictate a newsletter and have it transcribed. There are always creative solutions to get around any problem. The point is, make this process work for you.

# Section Five

## Putting It Together

# Section Five

## Putting It Together

Writing your newsletter is like writing to a pen pal or catching up with a long lost friend. Do you remember what it was like meeting up with a friend you hadn't seen in a long time? You talked until you caught up to present time. Only instead of one long lost friend, you happen to have a few hundred. Hey, once you start networking it doesn't take long to build up a huge network. Playing catch up with that many people is literally impossible unless they are all listening in to the same conversation at the same time. The difference here is that your intention is to deliberately stay in touch with everyone you meet and know. This isn't a "let's do lunch" and never scheduling the lunch. The masses do that every day. And you're not just anybody. You are a Million Dollar Networker and your newsletter is a tool of your trade. Let's start outlining the elements you are going to need to make a fantastic newsletter.

To make it easier, make a template so you don't have to reinvent the wheel every month. You can download one at www.YourMillionDollarNetworkBook.com. Your template should consist of a header at the top, a footer at the bottom, your picture in the top upper left corner below the header. You may choose to have a border or not, around the whole page. You can select from a two column or three column format or whatever suits your style. Next, transfer

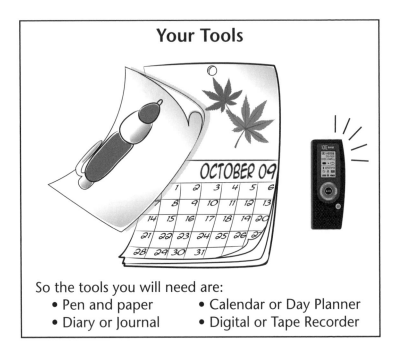

## Your Tools

So the tools you will need are:
- Pen and paper
- Diary or Journal
- Calendar or Day Planner
- Digital or Tape Recorder

the highlights of your month into the template. Use bullet points to keep it simple. Always "Save As" under a different name so you don't overwrite the master file. It takes just a few minutes at the end of each day or week to add notes to your newsletter. Then you're not overwhelmed with having to come up with ideas at the last minute, while staring at a blank page.

## Your Tools

There are a few basic tools you will need to get started. I have a daily appointment book where I write down my activities as they occur. This keeps the documentation of things in a neat and chronological order, and makes it far easier to sort out later. I also keep a success journal. I write down every win I have, in order to keep track of my successes. I keep it on my night stand and write in it whenever I feel like journalling. It's a great habit to develop. At the end of a great day, your mind relaxes as you can reflect on, and celebrate, the day's accomplishments. Reach over for your pen and your journal and write a sentence or two about your day. There is something therapeutic and cathartic about writing. It brings your thoughts to life. And as backup, I also have an electronic calendar to remind me of birthdays, anniversaries, holidays, vacations, business trips, seminars, insurance renewals, payment due dates and such.

On certain occasions, such as when I am driving, I carry my digital recorder to record my thoughts. This is a great way to remind yourself of important items that always seem to pop up when you don't have a pen and paper on hand. Once the thoughts are recorded, I have two options: transcribe it myself or have someone else transcribe it.

These are useful tools to help organize your thoughts. You will need an electronic word processing program in order to e-mail your newsletter. You can use any of a number of computer programs when designing your newsletter. Here are some examples:

### Microsoft Word or WordPerfect

These are the two most common word processing programs and come standard with almost all computers. You can design simple headers and footers, multiple column format like in a newspaper, then insert borders and pictures. It'll do the job.

### Graphic Programs—CorelDraw, Illustrator, Front Page

These software programs offer a more professional look and feel. They are not free, but they are worth considering. There is a learning curve involved, however you can do some pretty fancy graphic designs and give your newsletter a really polished look.

## Keep Your File Small

E-mailing a newsletter as a Microsoft Word attachment, especially with graphics, can end up making a large, one megabyte file. The document needs to be converted into a .pdf format. You will need the Adobe Acrobat program to convert files into .pdf.

People will need Adobe Reader to open this attachment, and the program is available as a free download at www. adobe.com. Your attachment becomes a read-only file which means the contents can't be tampered with.

### To convert to .pdf:
1.  Save your Microsoft Word document when it is finished
2.  Select File/Print (for Mac, select print/save as pdf)
3.  From the printer drop down menu, select Acrobat Distiller
4.  Print to the Distiller
5.  A separate Adobe pop-up window will appear with the .pdf version

### Text Only E-mail

Plain text e-mail newsletters are not easy to read. These are written in Word Pad, then copied and pasted directly into an e-mail. If you have no other way to distribute your newsletter, it is better to send it out in this format, rather than not send it out at all.

The key here is to keep your newsletter very short. It has to be no more than two mouse scrolls down. Preferably one. Separate your ideas with headers to create lots of white space. Be sure to save the best parts for the end, to entice your reader to scroll all the way down. This could be a riddle, joke of the month, coupon or a special offer.

## Use Adobe Acrobat to .pdf your file attachments

Adobe Acrobat is the program that converts a document into a picture of a page. It is a bit like a jpeg, which is a snapshot of your document page. It also prevents anyone from altering your newsletter. There are free versions of Adobe Reader on the internet that you can use to view a .pdf file. Pdf is a popular document viewing format because it enables your readers to view documents without having to buy the program. For example, if you were to create a newsletter in Illustrator and sent this file out to your network, they would need to have the Illustrator program installed on their computer in order to see it.

When installed, Adobe Acrobat acts like a printer. When you go to print your document, select from the drop-down menu instead, and select Acrobat Distiller to bypass your default printer. Then Voila! You're pdf'd.

If you are a Mac user, your instructions are just a little different. When using Microsoft Word, select print. On the bottom left hand side of the print window there is a button that says, save as .pdf. Just click it and save. You're pdf'd.

## For the Advanced User—Design A Newsletter

Html stands for hyper-text markup language. It looks and feels like your newsletter but there are no attachments to open. Html newsletters open up directly in your e-mail. The benefit of creating html versions is that it reduces the size of the e-mail, and eliminates the attachment since many computers now have spam filters that block attachments from reaching the Inbox.

Once you have chosen how you are going to format your newsletter, you can then start building your newsletter template. Since there are many ways to do this, I will lead you through what I think is the easiest way to get started. As I said in section four, if you find that another way works better for you, great! Go with what works best for you.

## Formatting Your Newsletter

Your smiling picture is the single most important feature of your newsletter. This is the very first thing your subscriber sees. Put your picture right at the top (left, center or right). Putting your picture on the left is most visually appealing to the brain. It records the image at a deeper level in your brain. You want your reader smiling back at you with instant recognition.

### Header: Title

Create a catchy title for your newsletter that reflects who you are and what you do. People will then start to recognize your header as part of your brand. Maintain a log of each issue for easy reference, such as Volume One, Issue One, Number One, along with the month and year. This will also help you remember which stories were used when. Occasionally you may wish to repeat a certain learning section and it's important that you know what date you used it last. It doesn't matter if you use Roman numerals or numbers, as long as you identify the volume and issue.

### Footer: Contact Information

This is where you enter your company name, address, telephone numbers, e-mail address and website. What good is a newsletter if people can't get a hold of you to send you business or pass on positive feedback? Remember that a newsletter can always be printed separately from the parent e-mail that sent it. If someone prints it out and passes it to a friend, how will their friend know how to find you? Even if it seems obvious, have your current contact information easy to find and easy to read. And don't use a really small font size for your contact information. It's too hard to read if it is small. It should be obvious and easy for your readers, and others, to find you.

## Font Size And Type

If your newsletter doesn't have a lot of content, why not choose a larger font size? Serif fonts are best with large point sizes because serifs help guide a reader's eyes in a straight line, and speed up reading. Serif fonts such as Times New Roman or Courier New are the ones with the curly letters. You can recognize them because they have short, light lines or curves called serifs projecting from the top or bottom of the main stroke of the letter.

If you have a lot of content for your newsletter, choose a smaller font size. Sans serif fonts such as Arial and Tahoma are best with the smaller point sizes. Sans serifs are fonts without the curly letters. When type is small, the cleaner fonts are easier to read. Make sure that you don't go below a size 10 font. You will be able to fit more words in the space, but it starts to get very hard to read.

## Create One, Two Or Three Columns

You can make your newsletter look as fancy or as plain as you like. This is your newsletter and will reflect your style. I like to use two columns for my newsletter. It is easy to read, looks neat and makes writing very simple. If you want something fancier, look at how other people design their newsletters. Copy whatever format you like and work with it until it reflects your own personal style. Keep in mind that the more columns you have, the smaller the font will have to be, and the less room you will have to write. It's also a good idea to be consistent from newsletter to newsletter, so think about it before you decide either way.

## Anchoring Photos

Have you ever attempted to insert a picture and every time you typed, the picture would move? This is how to anchor your picture in Microsoft Word so the text doesn't move around while you type. Insert the picture into the document first.

- Right-click on the picture

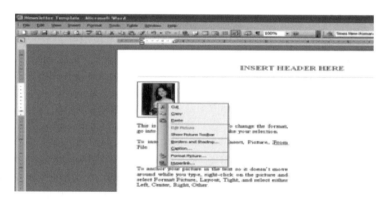

- Select Format Picture

• Select Layout

• Select Tight

• Select either Left, Center, Right, or Other

• Select OK

Your picture is now anchored. This means that you can now start typing and your picture will stay put. Play around with the different Format Picture menu tabs: Lines and Colours, Size, Layout, Picture, Text Box. Play around with a few techniques. If it doesn't work, there's always Edit/Undo.

## What Do I Write About In My Newsletter?

Okay, now that you have your header, footer and picture in place, let's get down to the business of writing your newsletter. An easy way to start is to take two minutes to share a success that you've had in the last month. It's a lot easier to do this with a partner. If you are alone, you can write, type or record your answer as you share out loud. Time it. You have two minutes starting right now. Don't think, just start writing. When your two minutes are up, then you can think about what you wrote. Until then, don't worry about it.

*Sometimes it's hard to get started with writing. One way to overcome writer's block is to ask yourself a series of questions.*

Everyone has experienced a success in the last 30 days. If you have a lot to choose from, select one that made the biggest impact. If you are searching for successes, then simplify. You are successfully reading this book. The ability to read is a blessing. There are thousands of illiterate people who cannot read. You can chunk this down to the most basic of functions. You are successfully breathing air easily and effortlessly. This is a marvelous biological function. There are people in the world who cannot breathe without an apparatus to aid them. Without the apparatus, they would die. For these people, breathing on their own would be a tremendous success.

Do you have ideas? You can share ideas. Do you have goals and aspirations? You can share your goals and aspirations. You *can* write. This is your moment—your time to inspire, inform and enlighten others with your writing so grab your keyboard and start writing!

Another great way to get started is to write out a list of gratitudes. What are you grateful for? Are you grateful for the air you breathe? The water you drink? The food you eat? The clothes you wear? The home you live in? The luxuries you own? The job you have or the place where you work? The people in your life? There is a never-ending list of things to be grateful for. Dig out your list, dust it off and share it.

What you write about will vary somewhat from month to month, but if you are overwhelmed by the idea of writing a whole newsletter, it really helps to have a structure that breaks it down into smaller, more manageable bits. Here is an excellent formula from Selena Cheung, that makes writing your newsletter a breeze.

## The 3–30–300 Formula For Effective Writing

There is a secret formula for writing an effective newsletter. If you cringe at the idea of trying to fill the whole page with content, use this simple formula and you will have a great newsletter in a jiffy! Just remember 3–30–300 which stands for:

- 3 stories
- 30 minutes
- 300 words maximum per story

This is a great formula to write your newsletter and it works every time. It's really a no-brainer, and once you get used to doing it this way, you might even find that the stories almost seem to write themselves. Having a time limit keeps you sharp and breaks the job down into manageable  pieces.

## 3 Stories for Each Newsletter

### Personal Editorial

The first story is your personal editorial. That means it's about you. Here is where you share your thoughts and inspire others. This is also where you can express yourself on a more personal level with an extended greeting, reminisce, or share about family and friends. If you are stuck for ideas, you might want to insert a success story or celebrate any wins you have had over the past month.

### Lesson Plan

The second story is your educational component or lesson plan. A lesson plan is a series of related topics about a whole. For example: as a real estate investor, it is important to educate your potential joint venture partners about the value of real estate. There are seven profit centers in real estate which can be shared over seven issues. Lesson plans create flow from issue to issue. Using them creates a theme and fosters an expectation from your readers. This portion can be a pre-written piece.

### Current Events:  Educate = Empower

The third story can be something relevant to today, or in the near future, that your readers can experience for themselves. Offer your readers something of value here, such as access to a free seminar or teleconference. Direct them to a blog or website full of valuable information and resources. Help them get in to a popular event with corporate rates. Tell them you'll be networking at a certain event and invite them along. Better yet, put on an event yourself. Provide access to as many freebie resources that you can. In this day of information overload, your readers are counting on you to sift through the data and distill it down to only the most valuable gems. They trust you to know what is important and what is meaningless data.

If you don't have access to free events yet, use this space to teach your readers something unique and special. For example, if you love quilting, you can enrich other people's lives by telling them how quilts first came to be, the different types of patterns, the generations of quilt patterns and the meanings behind the patterns. If you love hiking, teach people about outdoor safety or how to plan trips. If you love cooking, teach people how to use different kinds of spices in recipes. If you love health, teach people how to maintain optimum vitality. If you love real estate investing, teach people the economic fundamentals. Whatever you choose, be sure to engage and enroll them with your story.

## 30 Minutes To Write Your Newsletter

- Invest in a timer and when you are ready to write your newsletter, set it for 30 minutes

- Allocate 10 minutes per story so that you have time for each story.

When you limit your time to 30 minutes, psychologically the job will seem easier. If after 30 minutes you are feeling like you need a bit more time, take it. The whole idea of timing your writing is for you to understand that you don't need to spend hours on this. This is called managing your activities with a time limit. There really is no such thing as time management. We all have the same amount of time. It's how you allocate the activities you do within a certain time frame that determines how productive you are.

*Writing your newsletter takes practice. You get better and better with every issue until one day you realize how easily and effortlessly writing comes to you.*

## 300 Words Maximum Per Story

The average person's reading speed is between 200 to 300 words per minute. On the slow side, the average person takes 4.5 minutes to read a 900 word newsletter. On the fast side, it might take 3 minutes to read the same newsletter. This is why it is essential to keep your newsletter below 900 words to maintain that threshold for attention.

Each of your stories should be approximately 100 to 300 words long. A jam-packed newsletter with a 9 point type size contains about 900 words. A spacious newsletter with a 12 point type size contains just over 300 words.

Don't expect that each section will have the same amount of words. Some stories need more words than others. Use only as many words as you need. Don't go on and on because you want to fill the space. You will lose your readers that way. If one story is short, the next one may end up being longer. If you really need to bulk up a story, think about how you can add descriptive phrases that will engage the reader and get the message across in a clear and interesting way.

## Make It Interesting—Use VAK Words

In order to engage your readers in your stories, you need to speak their language. When you use words that resonate with your readers, they will hang on your every word. On the next page are some magic words to help spice up your newsletter. Use the three magic VAK words: Visual, Auditory and Kinesthetic, to keep your readers engaged.

### VAK Language = Read Me

There are three types of sentences to write in order to appeal to the majority of readers. They are Visual, Auditory and Kinesthetic. A visual reader likes to **see** words that appeal to their reading preference, words such as clear, clarity, perspective. An auditory reader likes to **hear** words that appeal to their reading preference, words such as buzz, ring, bell. A kinesthetic reader likes to **feel** words that appeal to their reading preference, words such as grasp, concrete, handle.

Use the list of VAK words on the following page to spice things up. Your writing style already reflects your preferred style. It will require a conscious effort on your part to include the other writing styles. Your task is to ensure that you are using visual, auditory and kinesthetic descriptive words at least once in every paragraph. VAK language will keep your readers happy and wanting to read more.

## How Do I Use VAK Words?

V = Visual. Visuals make up 40% of the population. To reach visual readers create a picture with seeing words. "I see what you mean. That appears crystal clear now. I get the picture." Using these visual words will instantly connect you to the visual readers.

A = Auditory. Auditory people make up 20% of the population. Auditory people search for sounds with hearing words. "That rings a bell. Here's the latest buzz. I'm all ears." If this resonates with you, then these auditory words make that connection.

K = Kinesthetic. Kinetics make up 40% of the population. There are two types of feelings: visceral and tactile. Visceral means gut feelings such as afraid or excited. Then there is Tactile, which is touch such as coarse or smooth. Create feelings with feeling words. "We need a concrete plan. Get a grip. Let's stay in touch." If these hook you up, then the kinesthetic readers get a handle on things. Isn't this exciting?

You will capture the majority of people's attention simply by using a visual, auditory or kinesthetic magic word in your story. Help your readers to see, hear and feel your story. This builds rapport with people because you are speaking a language that they are able to relate to.

Writing your newsletter takes practice. You will get better with every issue you write until one day you realize how easily and effortlessly writing comes to you. Whether you are surprised at your progress or not, be assured that change is a natural occurrence that takes place through time and repetition. Every day in every way you get better and better.

# VAK Words to Use

| Visual | Auditory | Kinesthetic (Feeling) |
|---|---|---|
| Appear | Accent | Balance |
| Appearance | Acoustic | Break |
| Blank | Announce | Catch on |
| Clarify | Ask | Cold |
| Clear | Attune | Concrete |
| Colorful | Audible | Contact |
| Crystal Clear | Be all ears | Feel |
| Dark | Be heard | Firm |
| Dawn | Buzz | Gentle |
| Dim | Cackle | Get a handle |
| Envision | Call Clear | Get hold of |
| Examine | Comment | Grab |
| Eye | Creak | Grasp |
| Flash | Cry | Hard |
| Focus | Deaf | Heavy |
| Foggy | Dialogue | Hit |
| Foresee | Discuss | Hold |
| Glimpse | Dissonance | Hot |
| Hazy | Dumb | Impression |
| Highlight | Echo | Jump |
| Illuminate | Growl | Make contact |
| Illusion | Harmonious | Pressure |
| Illustrate | Harmony | Rush |
| Imagine | Hear | Rough |
| Insight | Hum | Rub |
| Look | Listen | Run |
| Mirror | Loud | Scrape |
| Notice | Make music | Seize |
| Obscure | Melodious | Sensitive |
| Outlook | Monotonous | Sharp |
| Overshadow | Musical | Slip though |
| Overview | Mute | Smooth |
| Perceive | Outspoken | Soft |
| Perspective | Overtones | Slid |
| Picture | Pitch | Sticky |
| Preview | Proclaim | Stress |
| Reflect | Question | Stuck |
| Reveal | Quiet | Suffer |
| Scene | Remark | Tackle |
| See | Resonate | Tangible |
| Shine | Rhythm | Tap |
| Show | Ring | Tap into |
| Snap-shot | Rings a bell | Tension |
| Sparkle | Rumble | Throw out |
| Spotlight | Day | Tickle |
| Survey | Silence | Tight |
| Twinkle | Tell | Touch |
| View | Tone | Touch base |
| Visualize | Tune in/out | Turn around |
| Vivid | Unhearing | Vibrate |
| Watch | Vocal | Warm |

## Pictures = 1,000 Words

Use graphics and pictures strategically. Pictures create interest and encourage people to continue reading. If you use too many pictures, it will cause your newsletter to open up slowly in certain browsers. I use the three second rule. Send out a test newsletter to yourself or to a friend. If it takes longer than three seconds to open, your newsletter will most likely be deleted. The other option is to compress the image size so that they use up less memory space.

## The I To You Ratio: 1—I : 2—YOUs

It is natural for us to write in the first person. "I did this, I did that," and so on. However, an entire newsletter filled with "I" sentences is less than interesting to read because it's all about you. WSGAT? What's so great about that? Your readers are tuned into Station WIIFM: what's in it for me. Your task is to balance out your newsletter. For every sentence that starts with "I" you must follow with two "YOU" sentences. "YOU" sentences are inclusive, and allow your readers to see, hear, and feel that they are getting special attention.

## Remember: It's About You, Too

The most important topic of your newsletter is YOU. A newsletter isn't about just reporting facts. Facts don't create a relationship. Stories do. It's about your experiences, your feelings, your trials and tribulations, your values, your point of view. It's the way you talk to your friends. It's casual, intimate and informal. Make it an easy read.

You may choose to write in chronological order or not. The decision on how you want to do it will be your own. Find a system that works for you and be consistent with its use. People are more comfortable with predictability and it will go a long way towards building trust.

## Chronological Order

When recounting a situation, we tend to describe it in an after-the-fact manner. Help your audience experience the situation from a first-time perspective. Then they can feel what you felt vicariously. This type of description holds far more suspense and interest than merely recounting the facts.

## Transfer Your Diarized Information

Throughout the month, transfer the highlights of your day or week into your newsletter template and it will greatly reduce your writing time. Another way is to review your day planner and jot down the most significant events in your relationships, finances, or emotional life. Sometimes the simplest events in your life can make a huge impact on others. So write it down. If it made an impact on you, it might be helpful to others. It's your newsletter. You choose what goes in it and how it's organized.

## Expand Each Topic

When you have finished compiling your topics in point form, take a few minutes to expand each bullet point. As you near the end of the month (usually the last week), prioritize your list. Make a note of the items that aren't as important so if you run out of room, you can delete non-relevant topics to make room for the really good stuff.

## What It's Not About

When you feel compelled to mention, promote or advertise other people, products or services, be careful. It's easy to write about other people. It's safe territory. Remember, this is your newsletter—not theirs. Your subscribers want to know more about you, not someone else. Stay on topic and describe instead, how you felt about them, how they impacted you, and the lessons you learned from them. A personal experience is far more meaningful than a sales pitch.

## Use Hyperlinks To Other People's Websites

When you mention other people and their products or services, include their website in the story. Don't fall into the trap of going on and on about other people or their products. Just insert a link to their website. If your subscribers are interested, they will click on the link for more information.

Here are step-by-step instructions on how to create an embedded hyperlink in your .pdf document:

• With your newsletter .pdf file open, click on the chain link icon. This is the Link Tool. The mouse pointer changes into cross-hairs

• Locate the website text

• Use the mouse to anchor the cross-hair at the top left of the URL

• Hold the left button down on the mouse while you drag the box out to enclose the URL

- Let go of the mouse button. A black box forms around the URL and a Link Properties box appears
- Under Appearance/Type, click on the drop down arrow for the other option
- Select Invisible Rectangle

- Under Action/Type, click on the drop down arrow for more options
- Scroll down to World Wide Web Link
- An Edit URL button appears below
- Click on the Edit URL button

- Enter a URL for this link. You must use the full
    URL beginning with http://www.websitename.com
- Click on OK
- Click on Set Link
- Click on the Hand icon to return the file to
    normal view
- Save the file

Your website extensions are now hyperlinked! If you place the cursor over the link, the hand should change to a pointer finger. Click on the link to make sure it opens up to the correct web page. One wrong letter can make the link a dead end so be careful, and always test the links you have made. If you receive an error message when you click on the link, then check the website address to ensure that you have:

- Http:// at the beginning of the website URL
- The correct spelling of the domain name
- The correct domain extension such as .com, .net, etc.
- There are no spaces between letters or words

If you want, you can also hyperlink e-mail addresses as well as website URL's. This makes it easy for other people to send you a quick response. It's so much easier for them to just click on the link and have the correct address pop up in the e-mail.

To hyperlink an e-mail address, type the words "mailto:" with the colon in front of the e-mail address with no spaces, like this: mailto:july@onthebeacheducation.com

When someone places their cursor over the e-mail address in your document, the mouse pointer will change to an index finger. Clicking on it will cause the default mail program to automatically launch, with the e-mail address already

*Always ask permission before you send your newsletter to a new contact. Be respectful, ask first, otherwise you are spamming.*

inserted into the "to" field. A lot fewer e-mails will get lost in cyberspace if it is automatically addressed to you. Now wasn't that easy?

## What To Avoid

I quite often read I–I–me–me newsletters. The message is a resounding self-serving, "I am selling this," or "You simply must buy this from me!" Most of the time these newsletters are from people who are involved in a pushy organization, where it is all about sales. I wish they would stop trying to sell, sell, sell, and simply educate people on their products.

Education can arouse curiosity about a product, without ramming the sales down their throat. If your newsletter is just a sales pitch, people will not want to read it, or if they do, they will have to weed through the uncomfortable sell,

sell, sell, to get to the value. Whatever your product is, just educate people on the subject in general, don't sell.

Help people to become more aware. That way you become a source of knowledge. They will think, "Fred is an expert, he really knows about health. Maybe his product really is good. I'll give it a go." The thing is, you're not peddling your newsletter, so why endanger a potential $100,000 real estate investor on a $100 product? If they are interested, educate them first, then let them decide, by following a link in your newsletter to the product's website.

### Etiquette

Have you ever gotten a cc (carbon copy) e-mail? You are one of about 500 e-mail addresses on the same sting? Not only is this rude, your private e-mail address is now on the open market. On the web, there are robots and spiders that look for and acquire large blocks of e-mail addresses. The next thing you know, you are receiving spam from unknown sources. Simply send a polite e-mail back to this person and advise them to please remove your e-mail address or ask them at the very least, to use the bcc (blind carbon copy) function. If the e-mail was that important they could have e-mailed everyone on the list separately.

Before you send out your newsletter, make sure you have permission first. Unless of course, they requested to be placed into a group mailing list. Even so, their e-mail address should be protected from unauthorized users. Your reputation precedes you. The slightest provocation is all it takes to destroy the trust you have built. How you conduct yourself makes a big difference in how your network conducts itself towards you. Be courteous, manners count.

Your mission and vision have to be very clear to you. Most of the people in my database know that my mission is to bring value and inspire people. And if I can, I want to teach people to be financially free or empower them in some way—they like that. I know this because I have polled them and will continue to discover what else they like.

## How To Deal With Writer's Block

If you happen to get stuck and you think you have writer's block, ask yourself these four questions:

1. What would happen if I do have writer's block?
2. What would happen if I don't have writer's block?
3. What wouldn't happen if I have writer's block?
4. What wouldn't happen if I don't have writer's block?

That's right. If your mind went blank or is tied up in knots, that's just fine. Answer these four questions, and get back to your writing. Start a thought and the rest will come once you get your fingers moving.

Staring at a blank page will not stimulate your writing. Instead, ask yourself more questions. What kind of questions? Well there are all sorts of questions. For starters, ask yourself the 5W's + H: who, what, where, when, why and how?

- Who did I meet?
- What did I do?
- Where did I go?
- When is it going to happen?
- Why am I passionate about this?
- How am I going to do it?

The answers alone could fill an entire newsletter. Remember to journal the activities and highlights of your day and you will have a lot of things to write about.

### Words That No Longer Exist

In my opinion, "try" no longer exists in the English language or any other language for that matter. Whenever you hear yourself use the word "try," reframe the sentence without it. You will be amazed at how much more crisp and active your speech becomes. "Try" suggests something that may fail. Instead of saying, "I'll try to get it done by the end of the month," say instead "I'll get it done by the end of the month." Instead of saying, "Try it on and see how it feels," say instead, "Put it on and see how it feels."

I wonder if you noticed that I deliberately used the word "try" ten times, in the first portion of this book. People are comfortable with try, as it entails no effort.

Here are other flaky suspect words:

- Should have
- Would have
- Could have
- I'll try

Shoulda, coulda, woulda are wishful thinking words that do not exist in time or space. So why go there? Eliminate these words from your vocabulary and notice the shift from being tentative to direct. What message do you want to send out? Say what you mean directly, and stand by it.

## Too Much To Say?

If you think writing one page is an impossible task, after a few issues you will find that keeping your newsletter to one page will become the challenge. You'll be surprised at how much you actually have to share. And keeping it to one page is a must. You will lose your audience if you start to go past that.

If you have too much to say, you can always split your ideas over several issues and have your network begging for more. It's like a cliffhanger in the movies. They leave off just as the hero is in a life or death situation. Stay tuned for next week's episode.

Still having a tough time fitting it all onto one page? Reduce your margins (top, bottom, left, right) and font size to create more room. Leave enough white space to maintain a border.

## Sightseeing Is A Visual Feast

The human eye interprets pictures much better than typed words. Keep your pictures at a good size; not too big and not too small. Remember that pictures of people hold far more interest than pictures of things. If you must take pictures of things, then make sure you are in the photo to give perspective and relevance. For example, a picture of the Grand Canyon is breathtaking, but a picture alone cannot put this natural wonder into perspective. If you are in the frame, there is a better idea of scale.

## Distractions

Once your database starts growing, you will start to attract attention. You will soon encounter dozens of worthy causes clamoring for your attention—and mention—in your newsletter. A large network is an asset. People and organizations may tempt you with money, commissions, and referral fees to advertise in your newsletter. Once you start down that path for whatever the reason, your newsletter is lost. Your newsletter is never for sale or rent. You can highlight a person that inspired you or share the value you received at a certain workshop. Just don't sell out.

The purpose of your newsletter is to promote YOU, your life, your values, your challenges, your triumphs, your passions, your causes. Along the way, you add value to other people's lives with your insights and learnings. You accelerate the learning curve by helping others avoid mistakes that you've made or mistakes that others have made. You are unique and valued by your network.

## Benefits, Not Features

There is a big difference between benefits and features. You go to the store and there's a blender on sale. The salesman points out the features: it has 15 different speeds, maintenance-free blades, a 20 horsepower motor, yada-yada-yada . . . You go to another store and this salesman points out the same blender with these benefits: you can chop your food on the low speed or dice your food on the medium speed or enjoy a creamy smooth milkshake on the high speed. When you're finished, just rinse in hot water and your blender is clean in seconds. And because there is a lifetime warranty on the blades, you never have to worry about them wearing out. Who would you be more likely to buy the blender from?

Most businesses advertise the features of their product or service. The successful businesses advertise the benefits, and the successful networker provides benefits. We all have great features. Now focus on the benefits of knowing you.

## Show Yourself Professionally

I know it might seem like I am repeating myself, but get a professional headshot, instead of a portrait photograph. There is a difference. A professional headshot photographer is able to capture the essence of your personality. There is usually an interview process at the beginning so that the photographer can get to know you. The best headshot photographers work in the film and model industry. They all have a portfolio of their existing work. View their work first to see if you like their style. When you see a particular photograph that appeals to you, flag it and discuss with the photographer why you like that picture. If this is your first time interviewing photographers, view at least three portfolios before selecting your photographer.

Professional headshot photographers charge a sitting fee. They may take more than 72 shots in a single sitting. It is not unusual to find only one or two great shots. Most of the pictures will look posed and then a magic moment is captured in a beautiful, natural looking, shot. The nice thing is that you retain ownership of the negatives. It may be pricey but a good picture is a very good investment.

When you go to print off your headshots, make sure that you use a reprographic company that specializes in mass production of actor headshots. They have the best prices and will give you a product that you will be very happy with. In our digital world, pictures are brought to the printers on memory sticks. Ensure that you have a high quality photograph with a resolution of 300 dots per square inch (dpi).

If hiring a professional photographer is out of your range financially right now, you can always:

• Scan an existing photo to .jpg
• Take a new digital photograph of yourself
• Swap services with a professional headshot photographer

Your photograph is your calling card, it establishes rapport for you. You want your energy to be reflected in your photo. In the film and television industry, your headshot is more than your business card. Your headshot becomes your brand. What message are you conveying to the world?

Think about George Clooney. I recall a ruggedly handsome face with a slight tease as a smile. It's almost as if he's hiding something from you. It's his secret. It's compelling and it works for him. Now think about Audrey Hepburn. I recall her classic elegance from the movie *Breakfast At Tiffany's,* in the black evening gown, wearing a tiara. She radiated class and timeless beauty with a little dash of mischievousness.

What do you radiate? Class, fun or a teasing smile? Are you daring, authentic or thoughtful? Create a compelling brand through your personal image. Your picture becomes imbued with your attributes. Eventually your picture alone pretty much says it all.

## Wait Before You Click Send

It's a good policy to wait 24 hours after you have finished writing your first draft, so you can re-read what you wrote with fresh eyes, the next day. Then read it out loud and experience how it flows.

Sometimes you may discover a few long, run-on sentences. Other times what sounded great in your head didn't come out quite right. Our mind can leap from one concept to another and it makes perfect sense to us, while it leaves a big gap for outsiders. There are no inside jokes in a newsletter. Your thoughts must be inclusive. Nobody likes to feel left out of the loop. Also look for repeat tags on your sentences. Do you start off most of your sentences with "So, now this..." "So, now that..." Eliminate these filler words and make sure you vary the beginnings of your sentences for additional variety.

As additional back-up, I have a third party proofreader. If something is missing in my VAK language, the lack of it will come across loud and clear to the auditory reader; or feel cold and distant to the kinesthetic reader; or the visual reader just won't get the picture. Our desire is to create as great a sensory feast as we can. They can also spot if something is out of context. You want your newsletter to have a natural flow, so proofread. . . proofread. . . and proofread again.

## Spell Check / Grammar Check

This is your first draft. There may be spelling or grammatical errors. Spell check alone will not guarantee you error free copy. The reason that it is important to create accurate copy is that it reflects back on you. If you are prone to mistakes and overlook small errors, what other mistakes in other parts of your life are being overlooked? You see, how you do one thing in one area of your life often translates into how well you do in other areas of your life. That's a habit.

For example, one of my proteges was chronically late for appointments. It wasn't a big deal to her. She was only 5 or 10 minutes late. It became a big deal when this chronic habit spilled over into her being late for removing the subjects on a real estate transaction. The end result was a $5,000 loss and a hard lesson learned.

There are exceptions to the use of good English as mentioned in the story about Selena's first newsletter. Your readers have an expectation that your use of English will be somewhat "off" in your own unique way and they will make allowances for this. One of my Chinese proteges had a saying "I have a killing deal for you," which is her version of a "killer deal." It doesn't need correcting and it's uniquely her. However, do your best to make sure that your meaning is clear.

## Bad Spell Checking

Ifi u can read this than it is jst fin right? Wy botyhr to splel chk? I some times cant believe an assittent in this course. Oddly enough our brain can make sense of a few errors, but that is no reason to be sloppy!

*Have someone else proof your newsletter. It is amazing how easily others can seem to spot mistakes that we make.*

### Good Spelling

Is it easier to read when all of the words are spelled correctly? Well let's read it again, spelled correctly. *I sometimes can't believe that I am assisting in this course,* makes a lot more sense when it is spelled correctly.

Although the brain can make sense out of the words when we make a few typos, do pay attention to keeping your newsletter as free of typos as you can. Too many typos can lead people to think that you are sloppy and don't care about the fine details. This can lead them to think less of your abilities. Don't let your reputation suffer. Check your spelling very carefully.

## Proofread

Read your newsletter out loud slowly and thoroughly. Better yet, read it to someone else. Correct the sentences that sound awkward while you're reading it out loud. One trick is to read each sentence in stop action. I . . want . . to . . go . . The stop action of reading individual words helps you to notice if there are extra words or if something is missing from your sentence.

Another great way to proofread is to read it backwards. This works because it forces you to focus on one word at a time. You will be amazed at how many mistakes you find by reading backwards.

## Second Party Proof

Ask a trusted friend or colleague to proof your copy and to provide constructive feedback. Note that you are not asking for constructive criticism. There is no such thing as helpful criticism. Criticism diminishes. Ask for feedback instead. Feedback is helpful. Be thankful for their time, and don't take their opinions as law. Use your own judgement and if necessary, take their opinions with a grain of salt. You may choose to use their feedback or not—the ultimate authority on what to do is you.

## Read It Again

You may think that I am repeating myself far too many times with regards to proofing, but remember that haste makes waste. Never rush the newsletter out before it is ready. Once you have finished writing it, wait a day then read the newsletter out loud again. Is there heart in your stories? Can you feel the emotion? Can you picture in your mind's eye, what is happening? Do the stories ring true? How do they make you feel? Do they make you feel like you want to learn more? Do you feel like taking action after reading it? Have you inspired someone to look deeper into their life, their business or their finances?

A good newsletter evokes an emotional response engaging as many of the senses as possible. It also touches the reader in ways that changes how they view the world. It may be just a small change, or it may be an "Aha!" moment that gives them the courage to take a much needed action that will change the course of their life forever. That is the power of the written word.

# Section Six

## The Launch

# Section Six

## The Launch

Ladies and gentlemen, break out the champagne. You've made it to your launch day. This is the day that you announce your commitment to the world. And the world will be watching. This may be the most exciting and terrifying day of your life. Use the trick that actors employ—they acknowledge their fear, not to stifle it. Then they transmute the energy from fear into excitement. Energy is energy. It's how we use energy that differentiates people. We all get that tight feeling in our stomach—we call it butterflies—before a performance, a race or getting married. Get your butterflies to fly in formation.

Now it's time to celebrate! Channel any feelings of fear into celebration energy. Be loud and proud of yourself for moving to a new phase of networking, a new way of doing business. You have worked through your fears of writing and have something of value to share with your network. You may have even learned a few new computer tricks. Everything is in readiness; your newsletter is finished, you have proofed it, waited a day and now it's time to send it out to the world. This is exciting. You stand perched on the verge of a new adventure. One that will build you a million dollar network. Okay, so let's take those last few steps. There are only a few more things that you need to take care of.

## Organization Is Key

To make sure that everything is ready to send off, compile your address book and make sure it is completely up to date. In the days before computers, we did it the old-fashioned way, through collecting business cards or keeping a Rolodex. Find a system to organize and catalog your contacts, that works for you. There are various programs available such as:

- Outlook
- Access
- Maximizer
- ACT!
- Microsoft Excel
- Public Domain
- HyperOffice.com
- Constant Contact
- Goldmine
- SalesForce.com
- Act For Web
- Daylite

### Select Your Distribution Day

Pick a day of the month. It can be a specific day of each month such as the last day, the first day or any other day. It can be a week day such as the first Friday of every month or the last Saturday of every month. Choose your day and stick to it. Select your distribution schedule. Will it be once a month? Once every two months? Once every three months? Once every four months?

Remember that frequency is a factor of time and repetition so if you want to be front-of-mind, sending it out at the very least, once every 90 days, will ensure that they remember you. This is critical so choose carefully.

Weekly newsletters are perfect for paid subscription based services where timely information is important. For our purposes, weekly newsletters are too frequent, and may tend to annoy your readers. Be sure to let people know how often your newsletters will be arriving. And consistency is trust in action. It proves, through actions rather than words, that people can count on you.

## Compose Your E-mail Greeting

The very first message is the most important. It needs to sound like a personal message to a friend, not a generic greeting to an audience. It is a courtesy to let people know why you are sending your newsletter, and gives them the option to continue receiving it or not.

When I go to seminars, workshops or networking events, I let the person I meet know that I will be following up and that I will also send them a copy of my latest newsletter. I ask for permission first. If I do not receive permission in advance, then I go to my back-up plan. I insert a link to my website in the e-mail and invite them to subscribe to my newsletter. That way if they would like to stay in touch, they can click on the link and sign up for it on my website. It is an opt-in method that gives them the power to decide whether they find value in staying connected.

Here is a sample of how to word the e-mail:

Hello (insert their name),

It was delightful meeting you at the (insert event). Thank you for sharing your energy and enriching my life. As promised, I have attached a copy of my latest newsletter for your reading pleasure. This is how I stay connected to everyone I meet and know.

If you find value in keeping in touch, I invite you to subscribe to my newsletter at www.OnTheBeachEducation.com, as receiving future issues of *July News,* is permission based.

My mission is to inspire and empower the world to live in hope and victory, in order to create a global community based on collaboration, contribution and cooperation. I believe in world prosperity and peace, and believe that it starts with me first–you first. If I can help you, it would be my pleasure to serve you.

Cheers,

Yours Truly

For seminars and workshops where I am the keynote speaker, I have a slightly different strategy. I have a newsletter sign-up sheet. Save time and energy by making signing up easy. The composition e-mail is modified as follows:

Greetings (insert their name),

It was delightful to see, hear and meet you at the (event) at the (location of venue) last evening. Thank you for sharing your energy and enriching my life with your presence. In return, it is an honor and privilege to follow-up with you now. I hope that you received value and inspiration from my *Million Dollar Network* seminar.

I have subscribed you to *July News,* as your name was on the sign-up sheet. This is how I create value and stay connected to everyone I meet and know. You will receive a link to my free e-report "How To Turn Your House Into A Money Making Machine: Legally, Morally and Ethically," as my gift to you.

My mission is to inspire and empower the world to live in hope and victory, in order to create a global community based on collaboration, contribution and cooperation. All it takes is a plan and the know-how to implement the tools to create financial freedom.

Please let me know if you have questions or if I may be of assistance. Thank you again for showing up.

Cheers,

Yours Truly


## Attach The .pdf file

Once you've composed the e-mail greeting, attach the hyperlinked version of the .pdf file. Better yet, archive the .pdf file on your website (if you have one) and put the link in your greeting. This may seem redundant. It is offering your reader a choice to open the attachment or to view the newsletter on your website. Even if they viewed both the attachment and the website version, your reader just got two hits for the price of one e-mail.


## Html (Hypertext Markup Language)

Earlier, we talked about converting your newsletter into html. Although it requires some technical expertise, you can learn to do this yourself or hire someone to convert it for you. There are people and online businesses that offer this service. Html converts your newsletter into an e-mail compatible version including graphics, that allows it to open directly in the e-mail itself. There is no need to click on attachments, links or download anything.

### Addressing Your Newsletter

An effective newsletter campaign is addressed to specific individuals. Send your newsletter to each person individually or set yourself up with a contact management system that will send out your newsletters as if they were going to each person individually.

Do you ever get e-mails that are addressed to you personally and the message is a form letter? The e-mail is not addressed to "Dear Reader" or "Dear Subscriber." It has your name at the top. This is part of someone's mail merge, and although it may seem that they addressed you specifically, a computer grabbed your name and inserted it into the form letter. There is nothing personal about this type of e-mail. You feel special when they use your name, but they only addressed the message to you because psychologically, it works.

### Avoid Bulk E-mail/Spam

People know when they receive a bulk e-mail. Be unique. Be caring. Set yourself apart from other people's newsletters.

Be courteous and avoid spamming people. You've seen the bulk e-mail addresses in the cc (carbon copy) field. E-mail addresses are like phone numbers. Keep them private unless you receive permission to share their information. People do not appreciate having personal information spread around.

Remember to always use the bcc (blind carbon copy) field if you must send your newsletter as a group. This field hides e-mail addresses. However, anti-spam software and internet service providers are now filtering these types of messages from their system so that they don't reach their final destination. The key is being aware of internet etiquette and permission-based e-mail campaigns.

I am so serious about this that I used to cut, paste, attach, insert Hello So-and-So, then hit send, to over 1,500 e-mail addresses. This took about 10 hours in one sitting which I did on the last day of the month. After a few months of that, I switched over to the html version. It is not as time consuming.

## Permission Based E-mailing

These days it is no longer a courtesy but obligatory to ensure you respect other people's e-mail and prevent yourself being labeled a "spammer." Even though you may be e-mailing a contact or prospect who has given you permission, it is still a good policy to append your disclaimer at the bottom of every e-mail. Here is an example of what to say:

Please accept my sincere apologies if you feel you have been spammed by this e-mail. You are receiving this e-mail because we have met, shaken hands and exchanged business cards. If you would like to stop receiving e-mails from me, please reply with "Remove" in the Subject line and you will be promptly removed from my database.

If you would like my newsletter sent to a different e-mail address, please reply with "Redirect to new e-mail address" in the Subject Line and include your new e-mail address.

Privacy Policy: I respect and honor your privacy. (Your name or company) will never sell, barter or rent your e-mail address to any unauthorized third party.

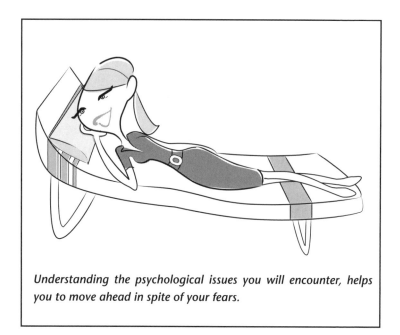

*Understanding the psychological issues you will encounter, helps you to move ahead in spite of your fears.*

## Psychology

As with any new venture, it is helpful to understand the psychological issues that you will encounter when you take this momentous step forward. This section is the main reason why most people do not have a newsletter or follow-up plan. Fear is psychological. Fear is emotional. Fear is *False Evidence Appearing Real.* Successful people use fear to their advantage. It's called acting in spite of fear. And the more you do it, the more confidence you build.

Did you know that you can actually build up your courage muscles? Courage is something that happens after the fact. You don't get courage before you do something new. It comes from experience and trust. Successful people know this. For example, if you desire a fantastic body that is lean, supple, flexible and strong, are you going to wait until you are lean, supple, flexible and strong before you start working out? I know this sounds silly but that's what unsuccessful people are thinking, whether they know it or not. They want proof in advance that it will work before they put in the effort. I'll get into shape first before I start working out. As you start working out, you begin to build muscles. As you start facing your fears, you begin to build your courage muscles.

Courage will grow as you move forward. So move towards your goal even if you don't have the courage. Trust that by moving towards your goal, you will gain courage.

Here are some strategies and tips that will help you gain confidence:

## Create a Praise Folder

Create an e-mail file folder titled "Praise" or "Good Stuff" or whatever feel-good title that works for you. When you receive positive responses from your network, do not discard these e-mails. Save them in your "Praise" folder.

Why? You will inevitably run across that one person with a negative attitude. I call them dream stealers. Their words will deflate you, depress you, and diminish you. It is hard to not be hurt by this type of feedback. It's not personal. It's really all about them. Life is a mirror. The words that come out of people's mouths reflects what is in their hearts. If you receive discouragement from someone, it is really a reflection of their life—not yours. So read your e-mail praises to remind yourself of all the people who appreciate you, encourage you and support you. Let the dream stealers go, and move forward.

I have hundreds of praise messages saved in my "Accolades" folder. These are the special messages that are truly uplifting for me to read. It's wonderful to read the beautiful words other people have to say. It is an amazing tonic for those

*Don't be afraid to delete people who are irritating, critical or constant complainers. If they don't appreciate your newsletter, let them go to make room for those who do.*

down days and it's a quick reminder of how special you are to other people.

## Cull Your Database

It's okay to delete people from your database. As you grow and expand your context, some people in your network may feel threatened by your progress. If a person rants at you, simply send an apology and express your regret for causing the inconvenience. Advise them kindly, that you will remove them promptly from your database.

The purpose of your newsletter is to build a strong network of success-minded people who are attracted to you. Keep your energy strong by surrounding yourself with good people. I call this seeding and weeding. You are weeding out the suspects. You are seeding the people who want to have a relationship with you. And the sooner you establish this with your existing database, the better. There are only two people that I have had to delete out of over 3,000 contacts.

## Conduct An Ask Campaign

One of the most powerful marketing tools is an "Ask Campaign." If you're wondering what your ideal client wants, then ask them.

Put out a query asking, "What is the single most important question you have about . . ." The query might relate to your specific skill, expertise, profession, hobby—or whatever it is that you believe is meaningful to your network. The responses will reveal the important issues. You will see the most frequently asked question. Now, all you have to do is respond to that need and your readers will be hooked.

There is a gentleman on the internet who had never written a book before, and wanted to write a best seller. He went on Google and asked what people wanted to know about a certain subject, then he wrote a book on it, based on the most frequently asked questions. It became an instant best seller! That is the secret to a successful newsletter. Find the burning questions and then answer them.

## Your Enrolling Vision

Take it to the next level and ask yourself this question: If money were no object and you had the resources of Oprah Winfrey, Bill Gates, Donald Trump, Richard Branson and Warren Buffet (five billionaires combined), what would you do . . . what would you build . . . what would you change in the world to make it a better place?

Most people think small. They stay inside their safe

little boxes. They lead boring, predictable lives that don't amount to much. They spend most of their time watching television and admiring people that have "The Vision" or "The Plan." Leaders enroll their supporters through their vision. It's like the Pied Piper playing a concert. Don't play it safe. Step outside your safe little box. Share your vision with the world, play your music to anyone who will listen, and watch how many people follow you.

## Your North Star

Your mission/vision statement acts like the North Star as you navigate through uncharted waters. It keeps you on course. Develop a personal and corporate mission statement or vision statement. Your mission is your specific purpose. Your vision is the big picture. Brainstorm using key word associations to start the process. Then keep refining the words until they form a clear and brief statement that sums it up.

Speak your truth. What makes your heart shine? What do you stand for? Let others take ownership of their opinions. Your vision/mission statement takes ownership of your own.

## Oscar-Winning Performances

In Hollywood, the Oscar is the highest form of praise for an artist's work. The best actors are able to convey their vulnerability to the audience, without appearing weak. Similarly, the best newsletters are written with a degree of openness and vulnerability. It's okay to be open and honest. We are human. We are all fallible. The victory comes in staying true to our hearts while empowering others to also become more authentic in the process. It's okay to get emotional. Emotions are compelling. Don't be afraid to express them. Be compelling.

Yes, I know this takes courage. But remember that courage is not the absence of fear. It's acting in spite of fear. You are more courageous than you know. Feel the fear and do it anyway.

One way to overcome fear is to procrastinate feeling it. Tell yourself you will deal with the fear next Saturday afternoon. Write it in your calendar and promise yourself that you will deal with it then. Most of the time, when the date actually comes, there is nothing to deal with. Psychologically, you gave it space to be. You accepted it, made room for it, and it disappears.

## What Happens Now?

After a while, your newsletter will become like one big marketing campaign. You will have built your brand around you, piece by piece. Your network will hang on your every word. They are your perfect target market. Let's face it. They are in your network because of similar values, attributes and tastes. Therefore, anything that you are interested in will also interest them. Wow! That's powerful branding and marketing.

Big corporations spend millions on advertising and promotion for this very purpose: to build brand awareness and to define a target market. Well, you've just accomplished that through time and repetition. So how do you monetize that? Very carefully and with a thorough marketing plan. Remember that if you fail to plan, you plan to fail.

The next section will give you an idea of what you need to look at if you want to make an even bigger impact.

# Section Seven

## Moving to
## The Next Level

# Section Seven

## What's Next?

For any business venture that you may embark on, you will need a marketing plan. Now that you've built your continuity program into a consistent, reliable and predictable cycle, you may want to look at how you can support your newsletter marketing efforts in conjunction with other communication methods. You can make it as simple or as complicated as you wish. Just make sure you have specific, measurable and quantifiable empirical data to compare your results to, and see how effective your campaigns are. For example, everyone who attends one of my seminars is asked how they found out about it so we can track where people are coming from. This is how I know that my newsletter is effective. Classified ads in newspapers have been a waste of money because not one person has ever shown up as a result of seeing my ads, whereas the people who subscribe to my newsletter or my network's newsletters, always show up.

It's easy to ignore an ad in a newspaper because you have no connection to it. You don't have a relationship with the person putting on the seminar, so how do you know it won't be a waste of time? If my network reads that I have a seminar coming up, they know there will be value for them.

## Your Marketing Program

A great marketing program is based on courtesy. The courtesy is in the follow-up and in adhering to strict protocols of conduct. This is where you can make or break your reputation. You can spend big money on glitzy marketing campaigns but it will all be for naught if you don't mind your manners, have a good understanding of business etiquette and the basics of energy exchange.

### Business Cards

One of the most basic parts of your marketing is your business card. It is often the first thing that people receive from you, and it tells them a lot about your company, and who you are. Because it represents you and your business, it is a good idea to have your business cards done professionally. There are business cards that scream, "I didn't care enough about this to spend any energy on doing it right," and there are business cards that call to you. You know the kind. They are the ones that you keep because something about them speaks to you. Let's face it, it's not very expensive to have business cards made up, with current print technology.

If money is an issue right now, you can design your own card in Microsoft Word and print it off on your own printer. The only drawback with these types of business cards is that they look like they were done on the cheap. You must have impeccable follow-up to overcome the "less than professional" impression you will make. A much better, and still inexpensive option, is to go to Vistaprint.com. You can get 250 business cards—as an introductory offer, for free. They also sell much more than just business cards.

Regardless of where you get your business cards done, make sure people are aware that you are a professional Real Estate Investor, as very few investors do this. You can

| CARD FRONT | Card Back *1,000* |
|---|---|

also put a number on the back of your card such as $500 or $1,000, hand it to the person upside down so all they see is the number, and say to them "This is your finder's fee if you introduce me to someone who purchases investment property from me." It's a very good trigger to help people remember who you are.

Like I mentioned earlier, make notes on the back of every business card to remind yourself:

- Date, time, place and event where you met them
- Phrase or word summarizing your conversation
- Brief description of the person, to jog your memory
- Important pets, significant other, children, etc.

If they mentioned it to you, then it's important to them. Your notes are life savers and you will be very glad you made them. For example, have you ever looked at a business card in a stack of cards about a week or two later and wondered who they were and where you met them? Even if you think you will remember them, a dull pencil is better than a sharp memory, so take notes. Be unique. Be diligent. Show people that you pay attention.

Of course, I usually write these notes after our meeting. If I must take notes during our meeting, then I kindly state "Excuse me. You're very important to me so if you don't mind I'd like to take notes so I don't forget our conversation."

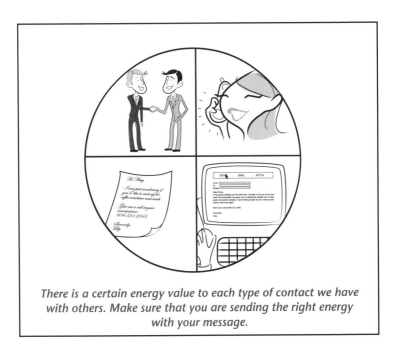

*There is a certain energy value to each type of contact we have with others. Make sure that you are sending the right energy with your message.*

This lets people know that you are not just randomly taking business cards. It demonstrates that you have made a connection with them and are interested in what is important to them.

## The Energy Cycle

Remember that everything is energy. Networking is energy— energy expended and energy received. Certain types of energy exchanges have a higher connection value because of the net residual impact of that connection. Meeting people in person and exchanging whole body energy is the highest form of connection. A physical interaction includes all the senses. You are imprinted by it.

When you can't meet in person, voice communication is almost as high. Your voice tonality and modulation have a greater affect on people than what you say. It's a great practice to learn how to effectively use your voice for positive influence. Keeping in contact is very important for building your relationship, and given today's high demands on time, you might not always be able to keep regular phone contact. In between telephone calls, people love receiving hand written cards and letters. The energy expended comes through in the time and thought it took to select the card or stationery, write the note, address the envelope, put a stamp on and mail it. I keep every hand written card and note I receive. I just can't throw them away.

Always use the highest level of connection value for your own benefit. For example, if you responded to a classified ad in the newspaper for employment with my company, I read your resume and your cover letter. Your qualifications meet my requirements and your letter is professionally written. You will make it past the first filter. Next I schedule a telephone interview. You have a pleasant telephone personality and you have all the right answers. You will make it past the second filter. Next we schedule the in-person interview. You arrive early; you are impeccably dressed; you display excellent interpersonal skills, and you charm your way through the third filter. That's working the hard way from the lowest net residual connection (a letter) to the highest (meeting in person).

Through your networking influence, you can cut directly to the third filter just from being referred to me by someone I respect and trust. That's because I have a degree of trust with their filtering process. Why spend the time jumping through hoops when you can save time and bypass the possibility of getting tripped up during the process I just described. Make sure that you always communicate using the method with the highest form of energy, when you want to connect with others. And get referred. It will save you time and energy.

## High Energy Communications Tools

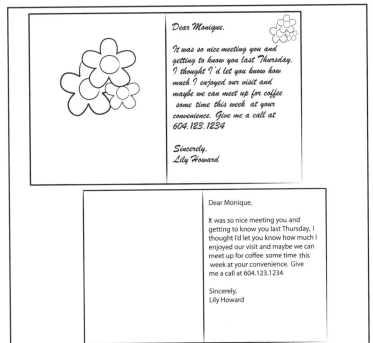

*Handwritten or handmade cards have a high amount of energy. Don't take the shortcut and send out typewritten cards. They lack energy and can come across as cold.*

### Communicating Via E-mail

The least effective form of connecting is by e-mail. It is probably the form that we use the most, and it is also the least effective when used as a means of connecting. The internet is a useful information and communication tool. However, you know how easy it is to misconstrue what someone is saying in an e-mail. You read something and you have no idea what their intention is for writing that sentence. There is no vocal inflection to go by or body language to give a hint. Is that sentence serious or playful? Is it harmful or innocent? This is why e-mail is best when used as a confirmation tool and not the sole means of communicating. You can use it to follow-up after a meeting or conversation and the context is already built in, so there is less chance for misunderstanding. Always strive to go for the highest energetic form of communication. It will reap rewards that you might never have expected. Only use the lesser energy methods if it's a matter of whether it will get done or not.

## Postcards

A handwritten card is always a special treat. People appreciate the time and effort it took for you to think of them. When you travel, always pick up a few cards to send to your clients. It lets them know that you were thinking of them while you were away. What better way to let them know that they are special to you? It takes just a few minutes, but can leave a positive lasting impression.

### Handwritten or Handmade Cards
- High energy
- People save them for weeks, sometime indefinitely
- Demonstrates that you care

### Typed Cards
- Dead energy
- May/may not save them
- Usually trashed

## Phone Calls

Start an A-list of the top 10, 20 or 30 people in your database. These are people who have invested with you before and are the most likely to do so again. Schedule a once a month telephone call to stay in verbal connection with them. Deliberately engage the connectors in your network even if all you do is leave a voice message. The time and energy that you spend on these connections pays off in huge dividends later on, in ways that you could never imagine. It's the little things, done well, that makes all the difference, such as the small gesture of saying hi, seeing your face, hearing your voice, feeling your handshake, making that connection . . . that is uniquely you.

Spend the time to keep your connections alive. It's a simple way of telling people that they are important to you and that you want to keep

Start a list of the people you admire and that you would like to have as mentors.

them in your life. It is telling them that they are valuable, and that they make a difference by simply being in your life. It creates a warm feeling and makes people want to give back to you.

While you are making lists, it's a good idea to start a list of the people you admire, and that you would like to have as mentors. Cultivate a relationship with each of them by telephone or e-mail. Remember, there's more energy exchange in a phone call than e-mail. Be sure to keep the conversations short—15 minutes or less. Make sure you are respectful of their time. Offer to help them with a project, become a volunteer or offer your assistance and support.

Mentors are people in demand and often get asked out for coffee, lunch and dinner. Other than sacrificing a few hours out of the goodness of their heart, make sure that you are providing value to them. Make it easy for a mentor to say yes to you, and you will benefit from their wisdom.

## Direct Mail

Direct mail is a form letter that is personally addressed to the recipient. Form letters are just that; impersonal, mass produced, junk mail. So keep the letter short, succinct, full of value and with a definitive call to action. Direct mail is not ineffective. That's why it's still a popular form of advertising and promotion. It just takes a lot more form letters going out to more people to get a response. It used to be that it took 7 repetitions before people would respond, but with information overloading our senses every day, it takes closer to 20 repetitions before someone will take action.

A letter campaign can be effective. People like opening mail that is addressed to them especially when it's not invoice related. Just make sure that it has a personal touch and doesn't read like a mass mailing.

## Radio

You can advertise on radio. A guerilla marketing technique for free radio advertising is to do a call-in give away for free tickets to a concert, a seminar, a cruise, a book, whatever the demographics of those listeners on that radio station are interested in. Always look for opportunities to use free radio advertising, whether that means you call in to radio shows as an informed listener or whether you arrange to be interviewed. Exposure counts.

## Print

Before you place a classified ad in the community, local, regional or national newspapers, study the demographics of who you are targeting and select the most appropriate print media. The ad copy should be educational based and not your typical buy and sell. Be different. Be cutting edge. You can offer to give away a free report: *7 Things You Must Know Before You Buy Real Estate,* or *How To Select A Moving*

*Company,* or *3 Things To Remember When You Buy Your Next Car.* You are providing value to the people who respond and in return you will have a higher rate of return for your effort.

## Billboards / Transit Shelters

This is a great way to target a local market including small signs or posters. There are public bulletin boards in your neighborhood. Make sure that if you are designing the ad yourself, that the text can be seen from at least 10 feet away. People need to understand at a glance, what your message is.

The words you use in your main title are the most important for grabbing attention. Keep this short and intriguing enough for people to want to continue reading. The sub-head has slightly more words and needs to be just as attention grabbing as the headline. Make sure your toll-free phone number or website is large enough to read from across the street. Have you ever seen a great ad and then couldn't find the website? You want to be seen and followed up on, so make it big.

## Website

The internet is here to stay. It is a powerful communication tool. This allows you to reach a global market or at the very least, allows your customers to get to know you on their own time. It is essential to have a website, especially when you are in business. Whether you hire someone to build it for you or you do it yourself, make sure you have a web presence. It adds a trust factor when people can find your business on the web.

And please make sure to set up an e-mail address with a website extension instead of using a public domain e-mail address such as Gmail, Yahoo, MSN or AOL. If you have a website address, it is easy to set up e-mail addresses that have your domain name as the extension. It is unprofessional to present yourself as a Professional Real Estate Investor or a business owner with a Hotmail account as your e-mail address. Let's look at some examples of how that looks.

amazingchick@hotmail.com **X**   don't go there

yourname@realinvestments.com √   professional

## Television

This is a premium venue for advertising because it goes to a very wide audience. Television campaigns work best in the context of an overall marketing strategy, and you need quite a large marketing budget to maintain and sustain a campaign. Mainstream television is beginning to lose its advertising power and is usually out of the reach of small business, but if you are able to get yourself known as an expert in your field, you can gain a lot of credibility if you are drawn upon as an expert. Many news shows look for people that they can call upon to give expert opinions in your field. Other opportunities come from talk shows. What can you talk about that is newsworthy?

Some cities have local programing that needs ongoing content. Get to know your local stations and find out how you can contribute.

YouTube and Creative Internet Strategies are beginning to attract more mainstream advertisers. Putting out your own interview on YouTube can capture a niche market, if you have an interesting clip. These clips can be e-mailed or spread through viral marketing, which is an excellent way to get known. Find new and creative ways to get your message out there.

*At every event you attend, put out a copy of your newsletter on the networking table, along with a sign-up sheet and a pen.*

## Events

A lot of events make networking tables available. Be sure to take advantage of these opportunities to create more exposure for yourself and grow your database. Put out your newsletter. Print off hard copies and put it out as a part of your marketing materials. Make sure to create a newsletter sign-up sheet and make it user friendly by having a good supply of pens so that there is always one on hand. Once people write their name and e-mail address on your sign-up sheet, that means you have their permission to contact them and send your newsletter. The sign-up sheet can be just a simple lined paper with a heading like this:

*Subscribe to July News at www.onthebeacheducation.com and get your free report! "How To Turn Your House Into*

*A Money-Making Machine: Legally Morally And Ethically."*
You will be surprised at how many people will sign-up to read what you have to say. And the great thing is, the people who sign up on the list have already given you permission to send them your newsletter. Your database has now grown, with very little effort.

## Seminars Or Tele-seminars

This is a great way to leverage your time. Instead of going out to events and meeting people one-on-one, create your own seminar and have people come to you. Live seminars are geographically restricted because you can only be in one place at a time. You can expand this limitation by having the seminar recorded and upload portions of it to your website. It can be a teaser for a future seminar, or an exciting clip that provides important information. Either way, it will add value to your website.

Tele-seminars and webinars don't convey the energy of your physical presence, but they are a great way to reach a large audience without having to leave your home. Another great idea is to have a copy of your tele-seminar available for download on your website. That way, if someone is not able to attend the seminar, they can go to your website and watch it, or they can send a link to a friend as a referral to you.

## E-mail (newsletter)

And of course your monthly newsletter is now part of your ongoing marketing campaign. This is one of the most cost effective methods of advertising available to you.

Measuring the effectiveness of your advertising and marketing is important especially if you're paying a lot of money for results. Keep track of numbers during a campaign. If there's little or no response, move to another mode. If there's great response, keep doing what works.

## Corporate Identity For Larger Databases

As your network grows beyond your immediate circle of influence, you may wish to consider protecting your personal information. Things to consider:

- Corporate website and e-mail address versus personal ISP e-mail address
- P.O. Box or Corporate Mail Drop versus your personal street address
- Toll Free Number such as www.Tagline.cc, versus your personal telephone number
- Corporate Mail Drop

What is a Corporate Mail Drop? There are businesses that rent out office space to small owner/operators. You don't even need to rent actual office space. These are known as virtual offices. You can rent a phone number and mailing address. You can find it listed under Office & Desk Space Rental Service in the telephone directory.

## Branding Your Business

Cathrine Levan, of KickStart Communications, specializes in corporate branding. She is as fanatical about branding as I am about following up. Here is her explanation about what branding is, and whether you should pursue it.

*Many people are confused about what branding is. Your brand is what you stand for. It expresses your personality and the promise you deliver. It defines the customers you want, and the ones you don't. In practical terms, it is a document that expresses the essence of your company, its vision, policies, practices, beliefs and character. Your brand should express the care that goes into what you do. A* good brand is easy to stick to because it stems from the inner core of your being.

Your company's brand should convey your values in such a way as to attract clients with similar values and needs. Branding is about creating connections that go beyond superficial attraction. It is about creating a bond with your customer that will last through good times and bad.

Good branding is essential for you to stand out, in whatever field you wish to excel. If you don't create a clear brand, it's like saying that who you are is not important. Who you are is important! By creating a memorable brand, you are making it possible for people to get to know you quicker, and build trust sooner.

> A good brand is easy to stick to because it stems from the very core of your being.

If you don't pay attention to your brand, you are still sending a message. The message is, "I don't care if my image doesn't match who I really am. I expect that you will look past my rough exterior and work hard to figure out what is real and what is not. Don't pay attention to what you see at first glance. Ignore it because it's not who I am." Is that really the message you want to send?

Well, for one thing, if you do that, you are making it pretty difficult for people to get to know you. Don't ignore how you appear in print or in person. How your business looks and how you dress, are ways in which you get to express who you really are. If you ignore this, people will make incorrect judgments about who you are. Wouldn't you rather have people make accurate assumptions right from the start? Otherwise you will spend a lot of time and energy correcting people's misconceptions. You can't ignore them, because they are future clients, that may avoid working with you because they don't have an accurate picture of who you really are.

*Most companies think that branding is about creating an image or logo that portrays a certain look. While this idea is part of the concept, it does not capture branding's complete essence. It's like saying that your clothing is who you are. It is an expression of who you are, but it's not the sum total of it.*

*Brand development is a process of discovery. Discovery of who you are and who you want to be. Discovery of who your customers are and what they aspire to become. It is a process that must be thought through with care and awareness, and once branding is done, it becomes the foundation of every piece of marketing material you ever produce.*

*It is a known fact that a well-branded company can charge up to 30% more than one that has not branded. So absolutely yes, do take the time to brand because it will pay off in increased corporate value, customer loyalty, higher income and an over all better customer fit.*

## Getting Noticed

Taking it to the next level is in the realm of public relations and using media savvy to garner free publicity. Local newspaper, radio and television media are constantly on the lookout for stories with a hook. People are bombarded with round-the-clock advertising and the noise is deafening. You know what I'm talking about. You have to block out the millions of consumer messages that bombard us every waking moment in order to function sanely every day. So here's the key to getting noticed. Use your low wattage message for high voltage impact. People are tired of pitches and promises that don't deliver. They want authentic, home-made, grassroots, street smart, real stuff from real people. That's you by the way. You are that quiet voice of reason and ration that stands out from the din of hype and hooey. Your newsletters earn you instant credibility. You have a database of contacts and a network of people that you have cultivated. You are a person of influence right now, whether you realize it or not. Most of us just don't take it to the next level.

Offer to write a column about your area of expertise in your local newspaper for free. Get yourself on talk radio. If you can't get on your local cable station, then videotape your own show and send it to the station. Get your message on You-Tube. You will be surprised at how many people spend hours watching clips.

Use your low wattage message for high voltage impact.

The great thing is that you don't have to do this on your own. Actually, it's imperative that you create a team who can support you. Create a strategy and then hire a publicist to implement that strategy. As Seth Godin puts it in his book, *Small Is The New Big, Conversations among the people in your marketplace happen whether you like it or not. Good marketing encourages the right sort of conversations. What people want is the extra, emotional bonus they get when they buy something they love."* You have the opportunity to be that extra emotional bonus for the people you meet and know.

## Taking It From Here

You are nearing the end of my book and you are probably thinking "Whew, that was a lot of really good advice, and I read it right to the end." This is not about you finishing the book! It's all about getting you started. Today . . . Right Now!

Unless you take action, your reading about and knowing how to start your continuity program is of no use. Knowledge is only good if you apply it. And don't avoid using your new found knowledge because you think you aren't talented or skilled enough to start. Go right back to Section Four now, and work through each step along with me. Don't get stressed about perfection. It's not supposed to be perfect. Remember, your newsletter is a work-in-progress because it actually works better that way.

Just start with where you are at, and share from your heart. Start with a sentence. It'll turn into a paragraph. Your first step will take you out of your comfort zone and that's normal. Use the 3–30–300 Formula to keep it simple. Then go back and check that you have your VAK words in each paragraph. And make sure to watch for the I:You sentence ratio. You can do it. I know you can.

Here are some suggestions to help you get started:
- Develop the habit of journalling at the end of each day
- Get a calendar/day planner
- Enroll a success partner to help you
- Copy a Newsletter Template in the appendix  or download the Microsoft Word template from my website at:
  http://www.YourMillionDollarNetworkBook.com
- Start today

Send your first newsletter to your immediate "circle of influence" and ask for feedback. Reflect on it, and don't obsess about it. Let's face it, there is no such thing as constructive criticism. Focus on how it can make your newsletter better. Through time and repetition, you will see the value of your network, and your net worth grow. Faster than you ever thought possible, you will have created *Your Million Dollar Network!*

# Appendix

## Resources

# Appendix

You will find all sorts of interesting goodies in the following pages. First, there is a list of interesting books that I highly recommend. No one book has it all, and within the pages of every book on this list, you will find information that will help you grow your business.

There are also samples of newsletters to inspire you into action. Some of them are my favorites and others are the favorite editions of the person who sent them out. Each has its own charm. Hopefully some of them will inspire you to create a newsletter that is uniquely yours.

Beside each newsletter I have included testimonials from people who have worked with me in the past. Sometimes it helps to hear from others, what their experience has been and how the information has changed their lives. It is extremely satisfying to receive the feedback from people, whose lives you have touched. It may sound corny but once you have your newsletter up and running, you will know exactly what I mean. Save your testimonials, they can provide others with much needed, second hand proof of your value and dependability, and they also serve to lift your spirits when you question your path.

## Recommended Reading

Gladwell, Malcolm: *The Tipping Point.* Time Warner Audiobooks, New York, NY, 2005.

Gladwell, Malcolm: *Blink.* Time Warner Audiobooks, New York, NY, 2005.

Godin, Seth: *Small Is The New Big.* Penguin Group, New York, NY, 2006.

Hill, Napoleon: *Think And Grow Rich.* Random House, New York, NY, 1988.

Hill, Napoleon: *The Master-Key To Riches.* Random House, New York, NY, 1982.

Jeffers, Susan: *Feel the Fear and Do it Anyway.* Ballantine Books, New York, NY, 1987.

Lublin, Jill: *Get Noticed Get Referrals.* McGraw-Hill, 2008.

Lublin, Jill; Levinson, Jay Conrad and Frishman, Rick: *Guerrilla Publicity.* Adams Media Corporation, 2002.

Mackay, Harvey: *Dig Your Well Before You're Thirsty.* Doubleday, New York, NY, 1997.

Port, Michael: *Book Yourself Solid.* John Wiley & Sons, Hoboken, NJ, 2006.

Port, Michael: *Beyond Booked Solid.* John Wiley & Sons, Hoboken, NJ, 2008.

Ruiz, Don Miguel: *The Four Agreements.* Amber Allen Publishing Inc., San Raphael, CA, 1997.

Sanders, Tim: *Love Is The Killer App.* Random House, New York, NY, 2002.

Wattles, Wallace D: *The Science of Success.* Sterling Publishing, New York, NY, 2007.

Widener, Chris: *The Art of Influence.* Doubleday, 2008. ISBN-10: 0385521030

## Great Websites to Visit:

www.dalecarnegie.ca

    get a free copy of Dale Carnegie's Golden Book

www.gitomer.com

www.harveymackay.com

www.michaelport.com

www.peterlegge.com

www.sethgodin.com

www.success.com

www.YourMillionDollarNetworkBook.com

## Testimonials & Newsletter Samples

### Selena Cheung, BBA, CMA

July, thanks so much for sharing and helping me. I sent my first newsletter to everyone in my network last night and I already have feedback from over ten people, most of whom really like my stories. I learned how to write my feelings and most importantly, how to market myself. What a powerful tool! I also got some e-mails asking me for mentorship on how to write newsletters.

I now use my *WealthyHome* e-newsletter to keep in contact with all of my friends. I have lots of people who are interested in investing with me and I refer them to my power team. I realized that by helping others, I was building priceless relationships. Relationships like this cannot be measured by money.

I quit my full time job in March 2006 and became a full time real estate investor and accountant. This was so exciting! Finally, I didn't have to work for other people and I have full control of my own time.

This has been a wonderful journey for me. July Ono believed in me even before I believed in myself. I have met so many people just like me who have a dream and want to live their life differently. Now I can help them or at least inspire them to find their passion. I know that I am going to continue sharing my dreams and my success with as many people as possible. And I know this is part of my life mission: to learn from others and give back to others.

*Wealthy Home Newsletter*
*www.wealthyhome.net*

# Wealthyhome Newsletter

JUN 2008

*Volume 36*

Wealthyhome Newsletter is now three years old! It's very exciting to have over 1,500 friends all over the world who receive this newsletter each month. This is really bringing us closer together. I have enjoyed receiving feedback from so many people, and your supportive emails have driven me to keep writing!

For me, the benefit of writing the newsletter is to keep me on track, demonstrate commitment, and share the ups and downs with my friends. I have found the most effective way to write is from the heart, as I believe this comes across and helps earn respect and trust from my friends. I also encourage my friends to write newsletter.

## ZERO DOWN PAYMENT – THAT'S RIGHT!
### *BUY AS MANY AS POSSIBLE*

I was in Edmonton earlier this month and, as you know, I'm a shopaholic. I love to buy real estate. This time I learned to buy property with ZERO down payment. Zero down is the program that banks currently offer if the property has a positive cashflow. The applicant has to meet the basic needs in order to qualify. This is one of the best ways to leverage your money, because your Return on Investment is almost infinite. (You still have to pay the legal fee in order to close the deal)

I found 2 properties with positive cashflow opportunity and made offers right away. In my case, I couldn't qualify for the program because I don't have a job. So I approached one of my JV partners and got him to qualify for the mortgage. With his excellent job, he was approved right away. This shows how there is opportunity to leverage other people's credit.

After I mentioned this Zero Down way to purchase real estate, I had three friends request to be on my next deal. They all have great jobs and we trust each other. This means I'll be busy buying real estate for the next few months.

There are always ways to buy property. You can even buy using other people's money (the Zero Down) or other people's credit. It takes creativity to be successful. Just ask yourself HOW, and you'll find the solutions.

## WEDDING PREPARATION UPDATE

The big day for Andy and I is fast approaching. After giving it some serious thought, I have decided to take a full month off before the wedding and to do something I always wanted to do. I have enrolled in a

4-week real estate course at Royal Mount College in Calgary. This will be fun for me to go back to school full time, stay on campus and learn more about something I am passionate about. It is a very special wedding gift for me to enjoy. See, I am so prepared for my coming wedding, that I can go back to school for a month!

Selena Cheung   Tel: 778-998-2888   E-mail: selena@wealthyhome.net

## Dave Watson

At eXtra Contact, we are sales & marketing strategists. We started doing a newsletter to keep in touch with our clients, pass them on monthly tips and reminders.

Our newsletter allowed us to keep in touch with everyone we met through our marketing and networking efforts. It's helped us find a use for all those business cards we collected! After a few e-mail campaigns we started getting calls from people we had met months ago wanting to find out more about our business.

We started recommending to our clients that they start a newsletter as well since one of the biggest pain points of our clients was with their struggles to follow-up with their prospects (97% of businesses will not follow-up with a prospect after the first month). Not knowing where to start, clients asked us to help them implement a newsletter for their business to enhance the sales & marketing strategies that were in place.

It then got to the point that e-mail marketing had become the focus of our business. E-mail marketing allows us to stay visual with our existing clients (more repeat business) and build credibility with our prospects so that we are "top of mind" when they are ready to use our services.

Overall, professional e-mail marketing, combined with sales & marketing strategies is a must for our business and has enhanced our existing marketing efforts tenfold!

*Creating Action*
www.eXtraContact.com

# 'Creating Action'
## ...From Your Database

eXtra Contact's
Email Marketing Tips
July 2008

### In this issue

Choosing the Right Subject Line

Include Your Staff in Your Marketing Plan Strategies

Success Stories: *"...highly recommend working the eXtra Contact..."*

Your Most Valuable Assset - Your Database

Contact Us

### Upcoming Events

eWomen Network

Thursday, July 17
**Accelerated Networking Luncheon**
Details & Registration

**Vancouver Board of Trade**
Events & Activities
*"I would love to invite you to an upcoming 'members only' event as my guest. If interested, please* contact Dave*."*

### Quick Links

**Constant Contact®**
TRY IT FREE
**Do-it-Yourself! Email Marketing**

Internet Marketing Free Report

'Evolution Chair'...
an Ergonomical choice

### Hi Dave,

One of the most important elements of your email communications is the subject line.

Next to the "from" address, the subject line will determine whether or not your email gets opened.

Each month we share with you powerful *Email Marketing Tips* to help you GROW your business! This month is focused on how to *Choosing the Right Subject Line.'*

**Networking/Marketing Tips,** provided by Gail Watson, of eWomen Network focuses in on *Including your staff in your marketing strategies.'*

As a member of the Vancouver Board of Trade, I would like to invite you to a *'Member's Only'* reception. Please contact me if you are interested.

*"What do you need to sell more?..."* Please contact us today for your complimentary 'Sales Action Work Sheet'... to help you sell more!

Looking forward to hearing from you. **Dave**

### Choosing the Right Subject Line

Writing a great subject line is no small challenge. You only have a few words to make it compelling, urgent, and specific... without sounding overly "salesy" or misleading your readers.

Here are some tips that will help you write subject lines that get great results.

**Keep it Short and Sweet** - Do your best to keep your subject lines under 50 characters, including spaces, as most email clients display 50 characters or less. Subject lines with 49 or fewer characters had open rates 12.5 percent higher than for those with 50 or more.

**Be Specific**
- A vague subject line is a waste of real estate. A great example of this that I see often is monthly newsletters with subject lines like, "The Green Thumb Newsletter: July 2008." This tells the receiver nothing about what they will find when they open the email and gives them very little reason to do so. A better approach for a newsletter like this is, "The Green Thumb: 3 Tips for Summer Gardening."

**Write it Last**
- Many email marketing services (including Constant Contact) prompt you to write your subject line first, as you are building your email. We encourage you to come back to it when you are done with your email content.

It's important to determine all the elements of your email first and then look for the most compelling topic to highlight in the subject line. When you are done with the body of your email, read it over and pick the "nugget" that will entice your readers to learn more by opening.

**Margaret Ferguson**

I am a Registered Physical Therapist, Licensed Seniors Fitness Instructor and a Shaklee Independent Distributor. For the past four years, July Ono has been a great mentor. Participating in her education program, I have learned the benefits of using networking and newsletters to expand my center of influence and to drive my business forward.

July encouraged me every step of the way. When I ran into technical difficulties, she was always at the other end of the computer to help me tweak my newsletter. She guided me through adding photos and was always willing to offer constructive feedback and formatting ideas.

To show how effective newsletters can be, I had numerous people come up to me at a week long business conference. While I may not have recognized a lot of them, they all recognized me from my photo, which is the first thing they see when my newsletter opens on their computer every month. They commented on various details they had noted in previous issues of my monthly newsletter, *Margaret's Stepping Forward*.

Thank you July!

*Margaret's Stepping Forward*
www.Shaklee.ca/MargaretFerguson

## MARGARET'S STEPPING FORWARD
Volume 4 Number 3 – March 2008

### Spring break
In this part of the country we already have spring. The daffodils are blooming, the ornamental cherry and plum trees are in full flower and some of the neighbours are mowing their lawns. My cats have decided it is time to shed their winter coats. It really is spring.

**Sulei** frequently sits on my lap with his head resting on my forearm. I look on this as additional weight training. Meanwhile my computer mouse is collecting hairballs.

In case you were in any doubt, the baby boomer generation is definitely having an impact on the fitness industry. There are a lot of people wanting to either maintain or improve their current health and fitness level. This is a good thing as the state of the health care or disease management system is shocking. A good friend recently had a total hip replacement. Years ago, she would have been discharged to a rehabilitation facility. Now she was sent home so has hired me as her personal home care Physicial Therapist.

### ICE'd
I am now **ICE**'d. That's the acronmyn used for the Instructor Compentency Evaluation. I have passed and am now also a qualified Fitness Instructor. I have been turned loose on the world as safe to teach seniors and Osteofit classes.

It was a very empowering experience to go to a job interview with the knowledge that I <u>chose</u> to work and <u>do not need</u> to work. It also does wonders for the ego when they called me and eagerly asked when I can start. The ink is barely dry on the evaluation papers. Now I can really give back to my community.

### Small world
Many know that my camera is never far from me at seminars. At my monthly **Real Estate Network Group (RENG)** meeting, I shared dinner with our very interesting speaker, **Tracy Piercy of MoneyMinding**. I mentioned that I would have to leave early to see my sponsored boy, Denis

of the Watoto choir. Tracy and husband, Joe, had billeted some of the choir a couple of days before and Watoto is also one of their favourite organizations.

One very valuable tip from Tracy, take small steps, a 1 degree turn repeated continually will eventually turn a bad situation into a better situation.

On May 2, 3 and 4th **Shaklee** highlights **National Women to women initiative (NWTWI)** Women's Health in the 21st Century will cover smart lifestyle and nutritional choices with particular attention to:
- Preconception
- Pregnancy
- Post-partum & Breastfeeding
- Perimenopause and Menopause

Raising Healthy Children in the 21st Century covers nutritional and lifestyle advice for:
- Infants & Toddlers, Pre-puberty Childhood
- Teens or Adolescents

The top 3 health concerns for kids of all ages:
- Childhood Obesity, Bone health and Immunity

For more info go to **www.nwtwi.org** or call me.

### Lessons learned
Time is truly more valuable than money. We can always earn more money. We will never have more time. We can chose to waste each day or use it for good purposes. What we chose to do each day is important as we are exchanging a day of our lives. Choose wisely.

**Email: margaretferguson@telus.net   Phone: 604-943-8603**
You never know what you are able to do until you step forward

## Maria Mitchell

I've been a part of July's real estate education program since September, 2006. Her meetings are filled with valuable information about real estate investing, with particular importance to believing in yourself. Believing that you can do anything you set out to do. It may not always be comfortable, but the doing is what keeps you moving forward.

Early on in the program she introduced us to a concept that seemed a bit foreign, or should I say intimidating. She encouraged us to create a monthly newsletter. Not being a writer, my first thought was how could I possibly come up with interesting things to share on a monthly basis? How am I going to capture and keep my audience's attention?

Although I resisted for a while and allowed excuses to prevent me from stepping up to the plate, I finally took the plunge and launched Maria's News. It initially started off as a quarterly publication, and has now become a monthly edition.

The focus of my newsletter is to share information on a variety of topics from real estate investing, to personal development. It's been so rewarding to have readers say that I've inspired them, and thank me for the information that I share each month. That keeps me committed.

My network has grown extensively and continues to grow. Thank you July for encouraging me to step outside my comfort zone, and helping me become the successful person that I am today.

*Maria's News*
*http://moneyminding.com/mariamitchell*

# Maria's News

**ISSUE NUMBER 6**                    **AUGUST, 2008**

## MoneyMinding

**Step 5** of the 12 revolving steps to Financial Independence. *Develop Saving and Giving Habits.* Consistently set aside 10% of all you earn. This money is not intended to fund a vacation, house, car, or, other consumer goods, but rather to put towards your long-term 'opportunity fund'. The goal is to ultimately get this money working for you! *How?* You may want to consider: real estate investments, private equity funds, limited partnerships, income producing stocks, and/or businesses. Before investing in anything ensure you know what you're buying. Attend local seminars on real estate, building businesses, or investing in the stock market.

Learn to create assets that return your money at a higher rate of speed and put money in your pocket. Keep in mind that investing is a team sport - make sure you have competent advisors.

*Giving* is just as important as saving. Even if you think you don't have enough money to give, we all have people and causes that are important to us. Create a giving fund of cash and a giving box of items. When charity is looking for support, you will be able to support their cause based on your alignment to their purpose.

*Action tip:* Figure out what you want to spend each month in order to live the life you desire while maintaining your true priorities, then look for ways to fund these 'planned expenditures'. For more about Moneyminding click here.

## The Smart Cookies

I had the pleasure of meeting the "Smart Cookies" at a recent networking event. The Smart Cookies are a group of five young savvy women with diverse backgrounds, who shared a common problem - consumer debt. Inspired by a 'Debt Diet' episode on Oprah, they formed a money club. They met weekly to discuss ways to pay down debt and attract more money in their lives. Their commitment to support each other along the way paid off 'big time'.

They shared their successes with Oprah, and in less than six months found themselves as guests on her show. Since then they have become media darlings.

To find out more about Katie, Robyn, Andrea, Angela, and Sandra click here.

### The 4-Hour Workweek

I recently read 'The 4-Hour Workweek by Timothy Ferriss. I enjoyed the book so much that I bought several copies to give away to family and friends. To summarize, in the briefest sense, it's about living and becoming more. If you want to be a part of the 'New Rich' and live your life by design now, instead of deferring it, you want to read this book. Included is an in-depth resource library filled with tools and tips - from books to websites that will help you navigate your way. If you want to double your income, cut your hours in half, or double the usual vacation time this is the book for you - I highly recommend it!

Maria Mitchell          E-mail: m.mitchell@shaw.ca          Tel. 604 - 418-3543

### What, Are You Kidding? . . . Me Writing A Newsletter?
Christian Gaulin

I don't even like to write, and on top of that, my English is not as good as my French! These thoughts were going on in my head as I listened to July Ono talk about the benefits of writing a real estate newsletter, a year ago.

I remember talking to July after her presentation, and within 5 minutes of our conversation, she challenged me to write my own newsletter in the next 48 hours. I had just joined her real estate education program a month before, so that felt like my *trial by fire*. Even if I had a lot of apprehensions, I took up the challenge. Within less than 48 hours, July received my first real estate newsletter titled "MAKE-IT-HAPPEN" Real Estate Investing.

The response from my family and friends was very positive and encouraging. Since that first issue in October 2007, I have written a newsletter every month without fail. My newsletter has been my way of sharing with my circle of family and friends, the news and tidbits about my real estate investing and other inspirational material that would be of value to them. I feel that over the past months my readers have been walking side by side with me on my journey in real estate investing. My stories about the purchase of my first two investment properties in Regina have sparked interest from some readers who liked my philosophy and approach to real estate investing. I am now in the middle of talks for joint venture partnerships.

My newsletter has been an amazing tool in my real estate investment business. I am thankful to July Ono for giving me that challenge, and I'm glad that I took it.

*Make-It-Happen Real Estate Investing Newsletter*
www.MakeItHappenRealEstate.wordpress.com

# MAKE- IT-HAPPEN REAL ESTATE INVESTING
## Newsletter

December 2007 - Issue 3

### Done Deal!

My wife and I have officially become owners of our first investment property in the city of Regina, Saskatchewan as of December 1st 2007. It is a great feeling. We have done it. And not without help from many people, particularly the Regina "power team" made up of Hazel, Denise, Annette, Kevin, Debbie and all who work with them.

### The Experience

Buying our first investment property was quite an experience. It involved going through 2 main phases: going to Regina to look at properties and the paperwork and negotiations after a property is selected.

We first went to Regina at the end of October to meet with our power team (realtor, mortgage broker, property manager, insurance broker and lawyer) and also to get a sense of the area. We were amazed at the number of houses that we could buy in the vicinity of $90,000 to $150,000. Being from Vancouver, it was hard to believe at first that decent-shaped houses actually existed in that price range! In the short time that we were there, we looked at 15 different properties, some better looking than others. We made 4 offers and got one. The other three were gone in a matter of hours.

It took from October 27th, the day we made the offer, to December 1st for all the paper work to get done. It started with an offer which was countered and which we then accepted. After the home inspection and after talking to the inspector, we asked for a price reduction which was finally met half way.

Meanwhile the mortgage broker was trying to find the best rate for us. Then the home insurance process started with the insurance broker.

Throughout all this, numerous communications took place back and forth through email, phone and fax. Then when we received the official documents finalizing the sale, we had to spend time going through the paperwork, struggling many times to make sense of the many technical and legal concepts and terminology. There were some moments when my wife and I wished one of us had chosen Law over Education and Statistics in university! When we were ready to sign, we had to do it with a lawyer in town since this is an out-of-province transaction.

After this great learning experience, it all makes much more sense now. We are excited to do it again, many times over. We will be purchasing more properties in Regina in 2008.

### Seven Profit Centers

Why does investing in real estate make so much sense? Because of the benefit of 7 profit centers. In other words there are not just 1 or 2 but SEVEN ways of making your money grow in this investment arena: EQUITY, LEVERAGE, CASH FLOW, PRINCIPAL, TAXES, APPRECIATION and REINVESTING.

**PROFIT CENTER #1:**

Equity is defined as Fair market value less debt service. The value of real estate inherently goes up in value over time. The ultimate goal is to buy a property for less than what it's worth; this gives you equity right on Day 1. One way to do this is to buy from motivated sellers who are willing to take less for their property. By purchasing real estate below appraised value, you achieve instant equity and increase your net worth. You also receive instant collateral with the bank. Over time, can you imagine how much equity you can build with your property!

### My New Year's Wish for All of You

Happiness deep down within.
Success in each facet of your life.
Family beside you.
Close and caring friends.
Health, inside you.
Love that never ends.

*Christian Gaulin*

211 – 620 8th Ave., New Westminster, BC    Ph: 604.525.3832    cmgaulin@telus.net

## Irene Dong, CGA

My newsletter, *Connext!on*, focuses on real estate investing and personal growth. It documents my journey to financial freedom and has inspired many people to reach their highest potential. Since I started writing this monthly newsletter in April of 2006, I have received numerous e-mails and phone calls telling me how much people love it. My friends appreciate that I am able to continuously keep in touch.

As a result of networking and building relationships the right way, my net worth has increased by more than 200%, and now I manage a real estate portfolio worth over $3,000,000.00. By sending out my newsletter every month, I have shown my readers and joint venture partners that I am consistent, committed and trustworthy.

When I applied the teachings of July, I became very conscious of my intentions and the messages I want to send to my readers. Therefore, I became more focused and concentrated my efforts on building wealth in real estate investing, and mentoring others. One of my readers recently said, *Connext!on* exudes love, joy and peace!"

Of course, it does make me feel empowered, and my confidence has definitely increased as a result of reading the feedback. If you would like to experience the magic of *Connext!on*, please e-mail me at Irene.Dong@yahoo.com, and get inspired!

*Connext!on*
http://irenedong.wordpress.com

# Conne)(t!on

Monthly Newsletter Issue 27, June 2008

**H!** The highlight of this month's events was the four-day FIC Invest-Fest. I saw so many people who have a thirst for knowledge and eager to invest for financial freedom.

### Trip to China – Part 3 (Shaoguan)

Shaoguan is the city that I was born in. It's a small city (according to Wikipedia, 2002 population is 3.1million), and many of the classmates I went to school with all found better jobs in bigger cities like Guangzhou and Shenzhen. I was often surprised when people recognized this small town, and this is because of its proximity to many highways and the major railway that connects northern and southern parts of China. This is the power of transportation effects!

Some may have heard of Shaoguan's Nan Hua Temple, which is supposedly the original place of Zen Buddhism about 1300 years ago. Nearby is Danxia Mountain, which is a famous scenic place I visited during one of my elementary school field trips. In addition, there are also many popular places for whitewater rafting and hot springs.

Last time I was in Shoguan, they were demolishing the building my first home was in. Somebody bought the land and buildings and was going to develop the area. These buildings were homes to hundreds of families. When I was in Grade 5, my family moved downtown to be closer to my father's new job and a better school. This time I only made time to visit my nanny's place, which is close to my old home. That neighbourhood has changed so much in the last 5 years that I could barely recognize it.

Besides several supermarkets that opened up in recent years, another big development is a new mall in Shaoguan. Before that there were no malls that have these nice clean spacious stores with fashionable decorations. Inside, I found boots selling around $200 Canadian after 50% discount. That's more than what the clerks are making per month! Clearly, there's a demand for luxury goods in Shaoguan too.

After May 31st, I earned those three letters after my name as I became a CGA. CGA represents 68,000 members and students in Canada, Bermuda, the Caribbean, Hong Kong and China. Qualified members can become a member of London-based Association of chartered Certified Accountants (ACCA) – the world's largest and fastest growing international accountancy body that has over 110,000 members and 260,000 students in 170 countries. That's great! I now have 438,000 accountants to network with!

The InvestFest conference attracted hundreds of investment specialists and investors from around Canada and the U.S. Local real estate investors and mentors, such as Selena Cheung, July Ono and Ozzie Jurock were invited to speak.

My favourite speaker is the leader of personal and professional development, Brian Tracy. He spoke for hours in the evening, but 9PM seems like 9AM to him. He was energetic, engaging and approachable. One of the most memorable stories he told is "Eat That Frog," his book with the same title that teaches others to stop procrastinating. He said if the first thing you do in the morning is to eat a live frog, it probably will be the worst thing you will do all day. He inspired me to tackle the most challenging task of the day, first thing in the morning and it has already made a great impact on my life. Thanks Brian! At the end, he signed his book, Maximum Achievement, for me and we had several pictures together.

The focus of the conference is U.S. real estate, and there're half a dozen speakers that talked about investing there. Would you like to hear BC millionaire, July Ono, and her U.S. team share with you the do's and don'ts of U.S. investing? RSVP here and I will see you on July 29th!

### Wellness Matters: Pick-Me-Up Dilemma: Pop vs. Coffee (Part 1)

Did you know not all caffeinated drinks are created equal? What is better when you decide to have pop or coffee for energy boost?

Did you know coffee contains polyphenols, antioxidants that reduce inflammation and protect again liver disease, heart disease and stroke? Pop does not have these benefits, and even worse off, the sugar mixes with bacteria in your mouth to form a mild acid that can lead to cavities. Sugary drinks also increase risk of obesity, hypertension and diabetes. Even diet or sugar-free pop has its dangers as a recent study showed regular consumption of either diet or regular pop led to increased rate of high blood pressure.

****

*"I am realistic - I expect miracles."*
*- Dr. Wayne W. Dyer*

*May your life be filled with love, happiness and abundance.*
Irene Dong 778-898-5860 Irene.Dong@yahoo.com
For events and announcements, please visit:
http://Calendar.yahoo.com/Irene.Dong

### Why Write A Newsletter . . .
Alice Brock, The Urban Shaman

Honestly, I almost hate to tell you how great publishing a monthly newsletter is for building a business. I want to smile serenely like a Buddha, and not let on about my secret marketing weapon.

When I first started my newsletter, I wanted to show off my expertise, promote a special or two, and get clients. And I am a little chagrined to say that worked. Holy cow! My client hours have easily doubled since publishing my first newsletter. In fact, every time I send one out, my client hours spike for two weeks afterwards.

But what has surprised me the most about publishing a newsletter, is how it connects me with my readers. Writing a monthly newsletter is a way to touch people, move people, help people, and make a difference in the world.

With a newsletter I can support my readers, educate them, inspire them, motivate them and tickle their curiosity.

A newsletter almost creates a business where there was nothing before. It gives you a presence in the world. If I had to choose one marketing tool to double my business in six months, publishing a newsletter wins hands down. But I wouldn't write a newsletter for the marketing as much as for the pleasure that a newsletter relationship brings me and my readers. When the pleasure is there, the marketing happens naturally and holistically in a way that feels right to your soul.

*The Angel Gazette*
www.AliceBrockShaman.com

```
* Welcome to The Angel Gazette! *

******************************************************************
IN THIS ISSUE: *Are You Hearing Things?* Clairaudience or
'clear hearing' is more common than you might think.  Read more
below.
******************************************************************

*The Angel Gazette*
An on-line newsletter for spiritual seekers who want to
awaken their inner wisdom to live an authentic and purposeful
life.

Alice Brock, Publisher
mailto:alice@alicebrockshaman.com
http://www.alicebrockshaman.com
Thursday, June 19, 2008
Volume 2, Issue 5

Published the third Thursday of every month

You've received this e-zine because we have met personally or
have contacted me by email. To leave this list, please see the
END of this e-mail.

Please pass on this issue to friends and associates - just keep
the entire message intact.


******************************************************************

IN THIS ISSUE:

1) A Personal Note from Alice

2) Success Story

3) What's Happening: *A Surprise and a Change*

4) Feature Article: *Are You Hearing Things?*

5) About Alice


******************************************************************

1) ** A PERSONAL NOTE FROM ALICE **

----------------------------------------------------------

June 19, 2008

A warm hello to you!

We just got back from Calgary, Alberta where we attended our
younger daughter's convocation (she received a Bachelor of Fine
Arts).  It was another poignant moment for me, this time as
```

### Heather Runje

About six months after I started my monthly newsletters, my girlfriend called to ask me to invest with her in a property. We met and I educated her on the seven profit centres. After that, we sought out a property to purchase together. During that time, she attended some courses on real estate and now a year and a half later she is one of the founding members of a real estate education and investment group. I have had numerous replies to my newsletter thanking me for the information and general comments about learning something new or just a great and enjoyable read it is. I have had a couple of friends ask me to introduce them to my next deal. Two other friends have become interested in real estate as an investment and have since purchased real estate for their residence and for a rental property.

I find it an invaluable tool to keep in touch with my friends around the world, rather than feeling guilty about not finding the time for monthly personalized correspondence to so many of them. This way they keep abreast of my interests and goings on. When I prepare the topics to write about, I enjoy reviewing my past month's activities to summarize my accomplishments, learnings and successes. It helps to keep me focused on my goals and plans. I am a private person by nature and every time I write my newsletter, I have a feeling of vulnerability, of exposing myself. I quickly overcome that by knowing that sharing and being open is a good thing and that being generous is rewarding.

*Tropical Musings*
www.CrewCaribbean.com

# Tropical Musings

Volume 2, Issue 6                    July 2008

Heather Runje
heatherrunje@shaw.ca
604-739-6139
Sea Connections Publishing
www.crewcaribbean.com

### Are you planning for Financial Independence ?

I would like to re-introduce myself to my readers. After my brother passed away 2 years ago, I felt my dreams were gone along with him, since my dreams were linked with his. We had planned to purchase property in Costa Rica. He left us in February before our April trip there. One of the many lessons through the transition was that I didn't need to let my dreams go, but re-adjust the means to attain them. I decided to pursue real estate investing. For 2 years I have been planning for my financial independence, have invested in real estate as one of my vehicles to get there and have studied with July Ono, BC Millionaire, Real Estate Investor and Educator in the RENG group. Is real estate a vehicle you would like to learn about? Please contact me, I would be happy to help you discover it.

### My Mom is Engaged !

Mom and Ken will marry in the fall.

## Another Real Estate Purchase !

### What are the benefits of Lease To Own deals ?

I close a lease to own real estate deal with a partner on July 30th. This is a great arrangement! We have found a tenant/buyer who is highly motivated to buy the single family home from us after 2 years. We have a lease agreement in place for the 2 years while they act as a tenant and pay for all maintenance during that time. We know exactly what our end payout/ROI will be because we have a set sale price in place. We are helping a family to own a home as they were not able to get the financing on their own. It's a win win situation.

### Buy Real Estate with Your RRSP Money !!

Recently I've gained the knowledge of how to go about using RRSP money to invest in Real Estate. It's simply a matter of paperwork and administration. Are your RRSP's gaining you enough interest or return on investment? Would you like to earn a higher rate of return than what you

are getting ? Why not accelerate the compounding of your RRSP investment and use it towards a real estate purchase ? One of the institutions/trustees that offers this RRSP mortgage is TD Waterhouse with an Arm's Length Mortgage. It must be paid out to a third party, no relationship through blood, marriage or adoption and must not be a company that you or a relative fully or partially own. If I have peaked your interest, please contact me and I'll be very happy to sit with you and show you just how easy it is to do.

Ready to start Real Estate Investing? Even if you do not have the means to do a full real estate deal on your own, ie; ability to get a mortgage, have a down payment deposit, or have the education and understanding to research the market, you still can participate in real estate deals passively. This will help you get into the market and start growing your portfolio.

Vacation Option! Consider House Swapping or Home Exchanges. Experience a new culture by living in it. Check out www.homeexchange.com or google it.

### Learn How to Buy US Real Estate !

I'll be attending this event held by July Ono, Real Estate Network Group founder. One of her US advisors will present about the 'right' way for Canadians to invest in the US, legally and for the best tax results. Tuesday July 29th, 7 to 9pm, Terminal City Club, 837 West Hastings Street, Vancouver. To sign up, click here.
There are many unfortunate foreclosure situations occurring in the US and people are losing their homes. I think that this is a prime opportunity to create win win situations with lease to own agreements.

### Tommy's Music

Tommy has been perfecting his songs for his first CD and has spent several days in the studio. He has a bit more to do including the final mix, and he's well on his way to completion. We will keep you posted. Here he is in the studio.

### Eric Choi

Who knew that reading a short, little newsletter would have been such a huge catalyst for so much in my life? I used to, and still do, receive a newsletter from a friend who developed into a very accomplished real estate investor. I used to look forward to reading about my friend's real estate and personal development successes each newsletter. I wanted that! And, now, I am doing that!

Reading someone else's newsletter got me started. I then joined the real estate education program founded by July Ono. Now, I am writing newsletters of my own. I am developing and maintaining relationships because of my newsletter, I am buying real estate, I am becoming a stronger, more confident, more successful person in every aspect of my life. I am achieving results with real estate investing and continuously setting new goals. Goals I never would have thought, were at all realistic before I met July Ono. And this is just the beginning.

My newsletter has been absolutely crucial from a real estate business perspective but also great from a social perspective as well. Just small words of encouragement from people who receive my newsletter have really been able to uplift me at times. Knowing people have forwarded my newsletter to others or hearing about people who would like to receive my newsletter gives me some pride that my newsletter is interesting to others and that my network is growing. And that the newsletter actually works! July's approach to newsletters and her entire approach to educating others about real estate investing, in my opinion, is second to none.

*Choices*
http://ericchoi1234.wordpress.com

# CH◉ICES

Volume 3, July 2008

It has been a busy and exciting last couple of months...

## MY FIRST INVESTMENT PROPERTY!

In early June, I went on a real estate tour of the Edmonton area put on by The Millionaire Diva group from Vancouver (http://www.themillionairediva.com/). I have been interested in the Edmonton market for awhile now, so this was a perfect opportunity for me to get a real sense of what the market is like there. We went through much of the Industrial Heartland (north of Edmonton) and saw first hand the industrial areas and development, met economic development directors of some municipalities, some members of my Edmonton Power Team, and many and much more! Thank you Millionaire Divas!

There's oil and much more in the Industrial Heartland.

After the tour, and after much evaluation, guess what? I bought a brand new 3 BR / 2 BA townhouse in Fort Saskatchewan, Alberta! My first investment property! It will finish being built later this summer.

## NETWORKING, MEETING SUCCESSFUL PEOPLE, AND MENTORS

Over this last six or seven months, I have been able to attend various seminars/events and meet various people who want to be successful and who are successful. You probably know the saying, it's "who you know, not what you know". Well, I have really come to appreciate and value that people I know really have affected what I know (particularly with respect to reaching my goals). Meeting these successful people and learning about how they approach life (both personally and with respect to making money) has taught me a lot, given me strength and confidence, and inspired me to continually take action

Millionaire July Ono (RENG) and me!

toward reaching my goals. I have been able to meet more and more successful people and millionaires through the power of networking and will continue to do so and develop stronger relationships with these people as well. As my mentors have told me, "it's all about relationships"!

Millionaire Chandan Toor (Millionaire Divas), Millionaire Selena Cheung (RENG), and me!

## PROFIT CENTRE #2 OF THE 7 PROFIT CENTRES OF REAL ESTATE

As mentioned in my last newsletter, there are 7 profit centres in real estate that make money.

1. Equity, 2. Leverage, 3. Cash Flow, 4. Principal Paydown, 5. Tax Benefits, 6. Appreciation, and 7. Re-invest Equity

This time I'd like to discuss *Leverage*. Leverage, with respect to real estate, is the ability to purchase expensive property with little or none of your own money. Compared to other investments, real estate investment has its benefits. For example, with $50,000, how much stock can you buy? Typically, you require 100% cash down and you can buy $50,000 of stock. At say a 6% yield on the $50,000 of stock, you would receive a $3,000 return on your investment (ROI). Now let's say you put that $50,000 to buy real estate as a 25% down payment on a $200,000 house. Again, with a 6% yield (this time on a $200,000 house), you would receive a $12,000 ROI.

In this very simplified example, the real estate investment would return four times what the stock market returned ($3,000 versus $12,000). In addition, against the equity in the house, you could go to the bank and borrow money to buy more real estate. You could not borrow money against your stock portfolio to buy real estate. You could use the margin in your portfolio to buy more stock but that can be a very risky proposition for most people.

"The only person you are destined to become is the person you decide to be." – Ralph Waldo Emerson

---

**Eric Choi,** Real Estate Investor

**Phone: 604.505.3461  E-mail:** ericchoi1234@gmail.com

### Alice Zhou

I am an event planner/publicist with a company called Gracious Host Events, in Vancouver, BC. I met July in 2004 at a seminar she was promoting. July and I instantly clicked and became a team. She taught me new ways about thinking positive, dealing with abusive people and creating consistent results.

It was July's brilliant idea for me to create a monthly newsletter. She was completely correct in thinking that losing contact with people you meet would mean the meeting was wasted; that is how *Social Butterfly Club* was started. When I started my company, I wanted to create a social club with many activities to bring the community together because newcomers to the city often find themselves lonely.

The *Social Butterfly Club* monthly newsletter started with me writing about the events I was doing, then I inserted tips I knew about event planning, public relations. The *Social Butterfly Club* has taken on more dimension over the past four years. Now the club is 4,000 members strong.

The best thing about July is she is not afraid of failure, and bravely faces them and moves on. Her attitude is contagious. If you're lucky enough to spend time with July, to hear stories of her past, you'll grow in admiration of her strength, and her accomplishments. I believe all her mentees around the world, are all her children. We will model her sense of adventure and provide unconditional love to others.

*Social Butterfly Club*
www.SocialButterflyClub.ca

Hi July,

**Social Butterfly Club Membership Contest**

This picture is Brandon Barton (my host) and Stacy Gibson (my assistant) and Brandon's friend, taken by Q Parker (www.quana.net) at the Playboy Party

We're currently looking for volunteers to help with the street promotion of Social Butterfly Club! We got very cool Social Butterfly Club T-shirts and Vests for men and women for fireworks night. Let me know if you want to be apart of the team, we'll put on a great volunteer thank you party afterward as reward.

**WIN A VIP NIGHT OUT FOR TWO!**

Open to current members by referring a friend to join the Social Butterfly Club and to new members that sign up between June 1 2008 – Sept 1 2008. Those who enter will receive a chance to win:

1) A couple's spa treatment at Dominelli International College of Esthetics ($200 value)
2) Star Limousine will be your mode of transportation for your whole VIP experience ($500 value)
3) Dinner for two at the Kentizen Restaurant in Tinseltown ($60 value)
4) Hotel stay for two at the Empire Landmark Hotel ( $300 value)

**June 2008 Newsletter**

**Cirque Du Soleil's Corteo Grand Opening**

# On The Beach Education® Corporation
## Product Order Form

Name: _____

Address: _____

City: _____Prov/State: _____

Country:_____Postal/Zip Code: _____

Phone: ( _____ ) _____E-mail:_____

Mail orders please send to:
PO Box 19056 RPO#16
Delta, BC  V4L 2P8  Canada

**For more information or to place an order today
Call or Fax Toll Free 1-866-340-2992  or E-mail
july@onthebeacheducation.com**

## Products

| Item | Price |
|------|-------|
| **Your Million Dollar Network** - paperback 192 pgs | 24.97 |
| **The Power Of Real Estate Home Study Course** A 12 module comprehensive program -includes the 7 profit centers of real estate, finding and analyzing the deal, 12 step money minding system 12 audio cds, and much more. | 997.00 |
| Total Order (Can $): | |

*Quantity discounts available upon request. Shipping/handling not included.*

Charge my _____Visa _____Mastercard

Card Number: _____

Exp Date: _____ Name on Card: _____

Signature: _____

**Please allow 4—6 weeks for delivery.**

# About The Author

July Ono went from $40,000 in debt to millionaire in less than 2 years, buying real estate with other people's money—and none of her own. She currently owns and manages a multi-million dollar real estate portfolio.

A real estate investor, educator and entrepreneur, July is the president of On The Beach Education® Corporation. Her company offers a coaching and mentoring program designed to take the fear out of real estate investing. Their goal is to help people leverage proven systems, to achieve their freedom day, sooner than later. Between 2006 and 2008, members have acquired over 38 million dollars of investment property.

She has a passion for networking and empowering others to live their potential. She strongly believes that applied knowledge is the path to enlightenment and financial independence.

July's single minded determination to succeed led her to develop systems and tools to help her clients succeed in business. On The Beach Education® Corporation was launched to help share her knowledge and discoveries with people who want to succeed in business.

July is a multi-talented woman with a host of interests that span from running marathons to screen writing.

She enjoys spending time in sunny Tsawwassen with her husband and life partner Steve Cain when they are not teaching seminars or traveling the world looking for new investment property.